IT'S ALL ABOUT LOVE–
reflections for women

by

Ruth Coulter

**Grosvenor House
Publishing Limited**

Scripture references indicated as NIV- Scripture taken from the Holy Bible, New International Version ®. NIV ®. Copyright © 1975, 1978, 1984 by International Bible Society. Used by permission of Zondervan Publishing House. All rights reserved.

Scripture references indicated as the Message - Scripture taken from THE MESSAGE. Copyright © 1993, 1994, 1995, 1996, 2000, 2001, 2002. Used by permission of NavPress Publishing Group.

Scripture quotations marked (NLT) are taken from the Holy Bible, New Living Translation, copyright © 1996. Used by permission of Tyndale House Publishers, Inc., Wheaton, Illinois 60189. All rights reserved.

Verses marked TLB are taken from The Living Bible, copyright © 1971. Used by permission of Tyndale House Publishers, Inc., Wheaton, Illinois 60189. All rights reserved.

Scripture quotations marked HCSB are taken from the Holman Christian Standard Bible ® Copyright © 1999, 2000, 2002, 2003 by Holman Bible Publishers. Used by permission. Holman Christian Standard Bible ®, Holman CSB ®, and HCSB ® are federally registered trademarks of Holman Bible Publishers.

Scripture references indicated as AMP- Scripture quotations taken from the Amplified ® Bible, Copyright © 1954, 1958, 1962, 1964, 1965, 1987 by The Lockman Foundation. Used by permission. (www.Lockman.org)

This book is published by
Grosvenor House Publishing Ltd
28-30 High Street, Guildford, Surrey, GU1 3HY.
www.grosvenorhousepublishing.co.uk

A CIP record for this book
is available from the British Library

ISBN 978-1-906210-50-2

To Rob,
My husband and best friend.
And to all our family and friends
Who were there for us
When times were dark.
You know who you are,
And I thank you from the bottom of my heart.

Acknowledgements

Special thanks to:

My wee daughter **Caris**
who made the lovely little heart
used on the cover

Mark Thompson
for the cover design

Joanne & Andy Taplin
for their encouragement

And to our Awesome God
who put these words
(and more importantly his love!)
into my heart.

Contents

CONTENTS

CONTENTS

Foreword

Ruth and I first met when we were thirteen years old. We both sat at the back of French class whispering to each other about anything that wasn't French. During our years at secondary school, we formed a deep friendship that grew out of our mutual faith in Jesus. We were also blessed with having a few teachers at our school that taught and encouraged us greatly in our faith. I often wonder if they know the incredible impact they have had on so many young Christian lives.

It was one of these teachers who first introduced me to Bible reading notes. I'd never seen anything like it before and it opened a whole new world to me! Going through my notes each day became something that formed part of my daily routine for years to come. Sometimes I wondered if anything was going in at all—but it wasn't until I was in my twenties and stopped doing them for a while, that I realised it wasn't so much that I missed 'doing the notes', but more that I was missing out on a regular connection with God, and I was definitely the worse off for it!

When Ruth first told me she was writing a book, I wasn't surprised as she's always been an encourager. It seemed that every time life was particularly difficult, a letter or card would arrive from her—seemingly out of the blue, but always incredibly appropriate.

Ruth told me the book was called 'It's All About Love.' She wanted it to be something that would be accessible and relevant to women, and she wanted to share God's amazing love with them. Often our lives are so busy that finding time to spend with God seems an impossible task. I know that for many of my friends and indeed myself, this often ends up with us feeling guilty about our seeming lack of effort. That's so not what God wants! We forget how much He just loves us to come and sit whenever we can—even if it's for just a few minutes— and hear how much He loves us, how wonderful He thinks we are and how much He values all the things we do at work, or at home for our families. These in themselves can be acts of worship to Him.

So, 'It's All About Love' is exactly that. I really hope and pray that this book refreshes you; that it helps you to see how loved you are, that you are a daughter of the King! Whether you dip in and out of it, or use it regularly as a devotional, I am convinced that God will bless you through this book!

Joanne Taplin

Preface

I've always loved writing! Way back in Cavehill Primary School I enjoyed writing poetry in Mrs McAllister's class. When I was 11, I hand-wrote a 100-page 'novel' about boarding school based on what I'd read in Enid Blyton's St Clare's and Mallory Towers series! Unfortunately I ripped it up sometime during my teenage years – I'm sure it would be hilarious to read now! I kept diaries when I was younger, and have kept a journal ever since I became a Christian in 1988.

This book began when I used writing as therapy after an episode of depression and anxiety. It was an attempt to focus my thoughts and to stop me worrying. But, I probably got most of my ideas when I was feeling 'hyper-happy' (hypomanic) and as a result, I was effectively 'banned' from writing for 2 years!

Then, when I was able to write again- I felt that I couldn't. I felt so unlovable, and unloving. I felt like a lousy Christian- and totally inadequate to be writing a book all about love.

I don't think this book would ever have been finished, if it hadn't been for Julie (Hammond) encouraging me to complete it last summer.

It has been written over the past 4 years- and as you will discover, not in chronological order! In fact, the very first section I wrote was 'Loving God means trusting His timing is best.' I got my inspiration while waiting for a coach back to Beauvais airport from Paris in Autumn 2003. It was published, almost as it appears now, as an article in Life Times magazine.

Some people say that everyone has a book inside them- it's getting it out that's the problem! They also say that giving birth to a book is almost as hard as giving birth to a baby! I guess it depends on whether or not you had an epidural!

A lot of this book is taken from things scribbled in my journals over the years. Often, especially when I was younger, I wrote down quotes I liked without proper references. I have tried my best with the references- but for many quotes, the exact location and even the author is unknown. If anyone can shed any light, please let me know!!

This book is really just an opportunity for me to share with you what God has taught me.

God has lavished His amazing, extravagant, everlasting love on us and we cannot keep it to ourselves. It must overflow to those around us – in our home first and foremost – then ripple out to affect all our circle of impact. Then, our husbands will feel valued, our children will feel accepted, our friends will be refreshed and all will see Jesus in us!

May this little book encourage you to be captivated by God's love, to revel in it, and pass it on!

PART 1

THE LOVE OF GOD

'God is love' (I John 4:16 -NIV)

The love God has for us

The love of God is boundless!

Readings – Psalm 8, Ephesians 3:14-21

When I was a student in Dundee, I used to go for 'stargazing stomps' down to Magdelene Green to clear my head. On many crisp, clear nights, I would stop and gaze at God's handiwork. It was awesome to look up and see the star-studded night sky. The heavenly splendour that stirred the shepherd David to write Psalms so long ago, like the one you've just read, gripped me. Yet, looking at the vast universe made me feel incredibly small. I was just one little speck on planet earth, which itself is only a part of just one solar system set in a vast galaxy.

> As David wrote –
> ' I look up at your macro-skies, dark and enormous,
> Your handmade sky-jewellery,
> Moon and stars mounted in their settings.
> Then I look at my micro-self and wonder,
> Why do you bother with us?
> Why take a second look our way?'
> (Psalm 8:3-4 – The Message)

In this day and age, as we strive to feel significant in the crowd, as we struggle with feelings of low self-esteem, we too may wonder why God bothers with us.

But any thoughts of insignificance should vanish when we consider our status. For though just part of creation, we are children of the Creator! His hands that set the stars in space, that flung the planets into orbit are holding us, and moulding us and keeping us in place! Wow! We should be overwhelmed by the present reality of God!

This Creator God is our very own God. He not only bothers with us, He loves us – He really, really loves us, with a deep, unfathomable agape love. We have been 'loved with everlasting love' (Jeremiah 1:3-NIV). 'God has poured His love into our hearts' (Romans 5:5-NIV)

Paul wrote 'And I pray that you, being rooted and established in love, may have power together with all the saints, to grasp how wide and long and high and deep is the love of Christ, and to know this love that surpasses knowledge – that you may be filled to the measure of all the fullness of God' (Ephesians 3:17-19 – NIV) David wrote 'Your love, O Lord, reaches to the heavens, your faithfulness to the skies. How priceless is your unfailing love!'   (Psalm 36:5 & 7 – NIV)

God's love is boundless. We will never fully grasp or understand it. It goes beyond our dimensions. It just can't be measured. It is so wide that it encompasses the whole world. It is so long that it can reach us just where we are, when we need to feel loved the most. Its height is higher than our highs and its depths are deeper than our downers! It is like a waterfall, deep and never ending from before time began to eternity!

Paul says 'May your roots go down deep into the soil of God's marvellous love' (Ephesians 3:17 NLT) May we draw nourishment and energy for daily life as we meditate on the awesome love God has for us.

'And I ask him that with both feet planted firmly on love, you'll be able to take in with all Christians the extravagant dimensions of Christ's love. Reach out and experience the breadth! Test its length! Plumb the depths! Rise to the heights! Live full lives, full in the fullness of God.'   (Ephesians 3:17-19 The Message)

'God can do anything you know – far more than you could ever imagine or guess or request in your wildest dreams! He does it not by pushing us around but by working within us, His Spirit deeply and gently within us'   (Ephesians 3:17- 20 – The Message)

The love of God is sacrificial

It was love that held Him there!

Reading: John 3:16-21

There's a famous painting that depicts Jesus on the cross, above the earth, in space. A closer look reveals that there are no nails in His hands or feet, illustrating the fact that it wasn't the nails that kept Him there. He could have summoned a host of angels to take Him away from the suffering but instead He chose to die for you and me – because of His love for us. In fact it's the greatest love, for 'Greater love has no one than this, that he lay down his life for his friends' (John 15:13 – NIV) 'God demonstrates his own love for us in this: While we were still sinners, Christ died for us'

(Rom 5:8 – NIV)

I used to have a little bookmark in my Bible that said: 'I asked Jesus, "How much do you love me?" "This much" he answered, and He stretched out His arms and died' 'This is how much God loved the world: He gave His Son, His one and only Son' (John 3:16 – The Message) The cross is God shouting through history how much He loves us! The crosss declares in blood red letters that God is love.

The prophet Isaiah was able to look down through the years and foresee the suffering the Messiah would

5

go through for us: 'He was pierced for our transgressions, he was crushed for our iniquities; the punishment that brought us peace was upon him, and by his
wounds we are healed. We all, like sheep, have gone
astray, each of us has turned to his own way; and the
Lord has laid on him the iniquity of us all'

(Isaiah 53:5&6 –NIV)

In love, Jesus left the glory of heaven to walk this
earth. In love, He hung on the cross, taking the punishment for our sin. In love, He redeemed us, paying for our
salvation with His own precious blood.

And the amazing thing is this –'He who did not spare
his own Son, but gave him up for us all – how will he not
also, along with him, graciously give us all things?'

(Romans 8:32 –NIV)

When I survey

When I survey the wondrous cross
On which the prince of glory died,
My richest gain I count but loss,
And pour contempt on all my pride.

Forbid it, Lord, that I should boast,
Save in the death of Christ my God:
All the vain things that charm me most,
I sacrifice them to His blood.

See from His head, His hands, His feet,
Sorrow and love flow mingled down;
Did e'er such love and sorrow meet,
Or thorns compose so rich a crown?

Were the whole realm of nature mine,
That were an offering far too small,
Love so amazing, so divine,
Demands my soul, my life, my all.

Isaac Watts (1674-1748)

'Thanks be to God for his indescribable gift!' (II Corinthians 9:15- NIV) 'a gift too wonderful for words'(NLT)

The love of God
means our past is forgiven

God's laundry room

Reading: Psalm 51

Nothing prepared me for the amount of laundry a small, newborn baby can generate! They go through so many little vests and sleep suits that the washing machine has to go on overdrive! And it just gets worse and worse, as they get older! Toddler's clothes just seem to attract dirt and dinner, and paint and muck! I suppose we shouldn't complain – at least we have washing machines!

I wonder how many of us need a trip to God's laundry room. The psalmist David wrote: 'Generous in love – God, give grace! Huge in mercy – wipe out my bad record. Scrub away my guilt, soak out my sins in your laundry. I know how bad I've been; my sins are staring me down' (Psalm 51:1-3 –The Message) 'Soak me in Your laundry and I'll come out clean, scrub me and I'll have a snow-white life'   (Psalm 51:7 – The Message)

For in God's eyes, the sin in our lives is much worse than the dirtiest of soiled baby clothes - 'We've sinned and kept at it so long! Is there any hope for us? Can we be saved? We're all sin-infected, sin-contaminated. Our best efforts are grease-stained rags' (Isaiah 64:5&6 – The

Message) 'For all have sinned and fall short of the glory of God' (Rom 3:23 – NIV)

When we come to God through Jesus and trust Him as our Saviour, He has promised to remove our sins – 'He does not treat us as our sins deserve or repay us according to our iniquities. For as high as the heavens are above the earth, so great is his love for those who fear him; as far as the east is from the west, so far has he removed our transgressions from us.'(Psalm 103:10-12 – NIV) All our sin, our failings and shortcomings are forgiven and forgotten because of God's great love for us. Our God says " I have swept away your offences like a cloud, your sins like the morning mist. Return to me, for I have redeemed you" (Isaiah 44:22 – NIV) 'Though your sins are like scarlet, they shall be as white as snow; though they are red as crimson, they shall be like wool' (Isaiah 1:18-NIV)

No sin, no matter how big it appears to us is too big to be forgiven. David wrote Psalm 51 after committing adultery with Bathsheba, then having her husband killed. (See II Samuel chapters 11&12) If we pour out our heart to God, 'if we confess our sins, he is faithful and just and will forgive us our sins and purify us from all unrighteousness" (I John 1:9 – NIV)

I like the start of a new year – a fresh start – a year as yet untouched and unblemished – like freshly fallen, pure white snow covered ground. Yet God's love gives us so much more than a new start in life – it gives us a new life to start when we trust in Him. We are new creations. We 'are not the same anymore, for the old life is gone. A new life has begun!' (II Corinthians 5:17 – NLT)

As we all know from experience, we don't stop falling short and messing up once we become Christians. We all have days when we feel like lousy mums and lousy Christians. 'I do not understand what I do. For what I want to do I do not do, but what I hate I do.'

(Romans 7:15 – NIV)

It's lovely to wake up to a winter wonderland! Everything is covered in snow and looks white and pure. Yet, a few hours later, it can become slushy and muddied by footprints. It's just the same in our lives. Although we are washed as white as snow, we become more like slush when we sin again. Just like our children's clothes, our lives get dirty again and we need many, many trips to God's laundry room to be cleaned – to be steeped in His awesome loving grace and mercy.

My 3 year old son hit his wee friend at coffee time in church. "Say sorry," I ordered. "Sorwee!" he said, flippantly. "No! Say sorry and mean it," I said. "Sorwee and mean it!" he retorted. It was hard to keep my face straight! Yet, how many of us need to say sorry to God and family and friends today, and really mean it.

Again and again we need to come before our God and ask for forgiveness. 'God, make a fresh start in me, shape a Genesis week from the chaos of my life. Don't throw me out with the trash, or fail to breathe holiness in me'

(Psalm 51:10 &11 – The Message)

May David's prayer be the prayer of our heart today: 'Create in me a clean heart, O God. Renew a right spirit within me. Do not banish me from your presence, and don't take your Holy Spirit from me. Restore to me again the joy of your salvation, and make me willing to obey you'   (Psalm 51:10-12 –NLT)

'Blessed is he whose transgressions are forgiven, whose sins are covered'   (Psalm 32:1 – NIV)

The love of God means today is for really living

Celebrate the moment!

Readings: Lamentations 3:22-26, Psalm 118

'Just a tiny little minute, only sixty seconds in it' But, it's the minutes that make up the hours. The hours turn into days and the days become weeks. The weeks make up the months on our calendars. The months mark the seasons, and so the year rolls round. The years blur as major life events, birthdays and anniversaries make landmarks in our lifetime.

In these 'wiping years' when we're wiping little bottoms, noses, faces and messes, it's easy to let the day go by in a blur of seemingly mundane tasks! We aren't able to see beyond the messy room, the endless dirty dishes and laundry. And we feel like we're going to scream if we hear "Mommee!" one more time! We merely exist, rather than truly living life as God intended it to be. It's easy to miss the point. It's easy to miss the wonder of these years when our children are growing, discovering and absorbing so much.

But, no matter what, the Bible says: 'This is the day the Lord has made; let us rejoice and be glad in it'

(Psalm 118:24-NIV)

On 1ˢᵗ September 2001, I took my 6-month-old baby daughter for a walk along Ballywalter Beach. It was a bright, sunny day. The tide was out and the water sparkled. It was the first day of the new school term. A woman stopped me to say, " Make the most of it! My baby has just started school!" And now, 5 years later, I wonder where the years in between have gone. Caris is now settled in primary school and the walk along the beach is just a nice memory. I'm just glad that I chose to go for a walk that day and didn't just get bogged down with the housework!

A Scandinavian proverb says: 'This day is a gift from God. What you do with it is your gift to Him'

Some one put it like this:
'Yesterday is history,
Tomorrow is a mystery,
Today is a gift,
That's why it's called the Present!'

Every new day is a fresh opportunity to experience God's love and mercy. 'The unfailing love of the Lord never ends! Great is His faithfulness; His mercies begin afresh each day' (Lamentations 3:22&23 –NLT) 'God has called us out of ho-hum mundane living to experience the abundant life'

Jesus said: "My purpose is to give life in all its fullness" (John 10:10 – NLT) "I came so they can have real and eternal life, more and better life than they ever dreamed of" (John 10: 10 –The Message)

We need to pray: 'Teach us to make the most of our time' (Psalm 90:12- NLT)

I was very challenged by something that Gloria Gaither said in an interview that was published by In Touch magazine in March 2001: "When your children are saying "Mommy, mommy" and you've got other things to do, I think you have to ask "Is there any eternity in it?" and give yourself away for things that last forever. A child is more eternal than a clean house...A calling builds itself into a calling out of a lot of days of regular stuff. There is eternity in every moment" [1]

Wow! Think about it-there is eternity in every moment, when we see those tiny little minutes from God's perspective! 'Everyday we stand on chords that vibrate throughout eternity' (Charles Finney)

We have got to 'Make the most of every opportunity' (Colossians 4:6-NIV) What we think is an interruption may be a divine appointment. Don't let opportunities pass you by because you think you know how your day should unfold! Listen to those inner promptings, and gentle nudges that come from the Holy Spirit. And remember, a coincidence is when God acts and decides to remain anonymous!

God wants our tiny little minutes, our days and our 24-7 lives to be given to Him.

'Take your everyday, ordinary life - your sleeping, eating, going-to-work, and walking-around life-and place it before God as an offering. Embracing what God does for you is the best thing you can do for him'

(Romans 12:1-The Message)

I probably don't need to remind you that just 10 days after that carefree walk on the beach, the unthinkable happened.11th September 2001. 9-11 is a date etched on our minds forever- the day that shook the world.

We truly don't know what tomorrow will bring. Tomorrow is guaranteed to no one. Tomorrow might never come.

I truly believe that God wants us to seize the day-Carpe Diem! What a difference it would make if we viewed our limited, precious time from God's perspective.

'Celebrate God all day, everyday' (Philippians 4:4-The Message)

'And whatever you do, whether in word or deed, do it all in the name of the Lord Jesus, giving thanks to God the Father through Him' (Colossians 3:17 – NIV)

'What you have done and created and loved in the Name of Jesus is all that will last' (Angela Thomas)[2]

We have this moment

Hold tight to the sound of the music of living,
Happy songs from the laughter of children at play;
Hold my hand as we run through
the sweet fragrant meadows,
Making mem'ries of what was today.

Tiny voice that I hear is my little girl calling
For daddy to hear just what she has to say;
And my little son running there by the hillside
May never be quite like today.

Tender words, gentle touch, and a good cup of coffee,
And someone that loves me and wants me to stay;

Hold them near while they're here,
and don't wait for tomorrow
To look back and wish for today.

Take the blue of the sky and the green of the forest
And the gold and the brown of the freshly mown hay,
Add the pale shades of spring and the circus of autumn,
And weave you a lovely today.

For we have this moment to hold in our hands
And to touch as it slips through our fingers like sand;
Yesterday's gone, and tomorrow may never come,
But we have this moment-today!

(Gloria Gaither)[3]

The love of God means our future is secure

Just trust- one day at a time

Readings: Psalm 25:1-10, Proverbs 3:5,6

It was 19th July 2002 - our 5th wedding anniversary and I felt like I was the happiest person on the planet! We were on holiday by Lake Orta, one of the smaller Italian lakes. Caris, our 18 month old toddler was asleep in the cot, Rob was having a siesta and I was sitting out on the balcony. The sunshine was making the lake shimmer below. Bright red geraniums were bursting out of window boxes all around. Birds were singing & life was beautiful! I was reading, reflecting, scribbling in my journal and thanking God for all his blessings over the previous 5 years. I was thanking him for the baby, yet unborn, growing inside of me. I just felt so blessed.

I was looking forward in anticipation to the next 5 years, wondering what lay ahead, asking God to guide us-as a couple and as a growing family.

Someone said that it's just as well that we don't know what lies around the corner-and it is! If someone, anyone, an angel-or God Himself had revealed that day what the future held for us in the next few years, I don't think that I would have been able to get up of my chair- and I certainly wouldn't have got on the plane home! For the next 3 years were the most difficult of my life so far.

A few months later, I woke suddenly in the middle of the night, and heard God's voice say, in a more real way than ever before, "Don't be afraid, for I am with you" As Christians, we don't need to fear- no matter what - for our Father God is with us, through it all.

Our future is not random or haphazard. Our loving Heavenly father who knows what is best for us has planned it. "For I know the plans I have for you", declares the Lord, "plans to prosper you and not to harm you, plans to give you hope and a future"

(Jeremiah 29:11 –NIV)

Often we worry about what the future holds, but we shouldn't. After all, today is the tomorrow we worried about yesterday! We must just trust. 'God is not asking you to have your whole future figured out. He is asking you to trust that He has your future planned' (Stormie Omartian)[4]

Our future happens just one day at a time & He gives 'just enough light for the step I'm on!'(as the title of one of Stormie Omartian's books reminds us) And no matter what, He is in control.

When I was a teenager, my Granda Murphy always wrote Proverbs 3:5&6 on my birthday cards, as a reminder that I should trust God, rather than my own instincts, and that I should seek Him first for guidance. The day I got my A level results, these verses 'just happened' to be my daily reading. I'd spent most of the day in tears as I hadn't got the grades for Queen's University Belfast. These verses reminded me to just trust. Looking back I realise that it was God's plan for me to study in Dundee for five years! And if I had went to

Queen's, I wouldn't have met Rob and many other great friends, and I would have missed out on all the craic of living away from home!

I like the way the Message paraphrases those verses: 'Trust God from the bottom of your heart; don't try to figure out everything on your own. Listen for God's voice in everything you do, everywhere you go; he's the one who will keep you on track'

(Proverbs 3:5&6 The Message)

God is charting our path. 'You chart the path ahead of me and tell me where to stop and rest. Every moment you know where I am. You both precede and follow me. You place your hand of blessing on my head' (Psalm 139:3&5 – NLT) He goes before us- 'The Lord Himself goes before you and will be with you; he will never leave you nor forsake you. Do not be afraid; do not be discouraged' (Deuteronomy 31:8 – NIV) And He goes with us – 'Be strong and courageous. Do not be afraid or terrified because of them, for the Lord Your God goes with you; he will never leave you nor forsake you'

(Deuteronomy 31:6 – NIV)

Our destiny is in His hands. He knows the way that we take and He leads by quiet waters and green pastures, through mountains and valleys and the storms of life. As God of the universe, He holds our future. And as Abba, Father, He holds our hand.

Corrie ten Boom's father told her: "When Jesus takes your hand, he keeps you close. When Jesus keeps you close, He leads you through your whole life. When Jesus leads you through your whole life, He brings you safely home" Step by step He'll lead us all the way home.

'For this God is our God forever and ever; he will be our guide, even to the end.' (Psalm 48:14 NIV)

'You will keep on guiding me with your counsel, leading me to a glorious destiny' (Psalm 73:24 NLT) We have an inheritance kept in heaven for us.

'But from everlasting to everlasting the Lord's love is with those who fear Him' (Psalm 103:17 – NIV) His love stretches from eternity past and never ends.

'You have a place in God's plan that no-one else can fill-and it's running over with blessings only **He** can give' (Day Spring Cards)[5]

Settle with the past.
Engage with the present.
Believe in the future.

The love of God means we are daughters of the King

Children of God!

Readings: Psalm 139, Ephesians 1:3-14

Every mother knows that no two children are the same – siblings and even identical twins have their different personalities and temperaments. We are all unique – from our fingerprints to our attitudes toward life. The differences can be apparent even before birth. At my 20 week scans, the different personalities of my two children were evident! Caris wouldn't lie still long enough for the ultrasonographer to do measurements, while Ethan was lying calm and relaxed. Today, Caris is a very lively 3 year old – a real go – getter who doesn't stay in the one spot too long, while Ethan is much more laid back and mellow (like his dad!)

I have a scan picture of both Caris and Ethan in my Bible. On the back, I've written these words from Psalm 139: 'You made all the delicate, inner parts of my body, and knit them together in my mother's womb. Thank you for making me so wonderfully complex! It is amazing to think about. Your workmanship is marvellous – and how well I know it. You were there while I was being formed in utter seclusion! You saw me before I was born and scheduled each day of my life before I began to breathe. Every day was recorded in Your Book!' (Psalm 139:13-16 TLB)

Before each of us was born, God was there watching over us. He was involved while we were being 'fearfully and wonderfully made' in His image. 'Long before he had laid down earth's foundations, he had us in mind, had settled on us as the focus of his love, to be made whole and holy by his love' (Ephesians 1:4 The Message) 'His unchanging plan has always been to adopt us into his own family by bringing us to himself through Jesus Christ. And this gave him great pleasure' (Ephesians 1:5 NLT) 'For he chose us in him before the creation of the world to be holy and blameless in his sight. In love he predestined us to be adopted as his sons through Jesus Christ, in accordance with his pleasure and will – to the praise of his glorious grace, which he has freely given us in the One he loves' (Ephesians 1:4-6 – NIV)

The Father heart of God is present in the pages of both the Old and New Testament. God said 'As a mother comforts her child so I will comfort you' (Isaiah 66:13-NIV) He lovingly protects us 'like an eagle that stirs up its nests and hovers over its young, and spreads its wings to protect them and carries them on its pinions' (Deuteronomy 32:11 – NIV) 'He will cover you with his feathers, and under his wings you will find refuge' (Psalm 91:4 – NIV)

God's parenting goes far beyond our human expectations and experiences. Although a mother can sometimes forget the child she bore, God cannot and will not forget us (Isaiah 49:14&15) Our names are engraved on His palms – His nail pierced hands. (Isaiah 49:16) God 'will take great delight in you, he will quiet you with his love, he will rejoice over you with singing'

(Zephaniah 3:17 -NIV) For the amazing thing is this: 'Yet to all who received him, to those who believed in his name, he gave the right to become children of God' (John1:12 – NIV) We are born of God and adopted into His family! Wow! We are daughters of the Almighty God, the King of kings!

'But you have received the spirit of sonship. And by him we cry "Abba, Father"(Romans 8:15 – NIV) God is not a strict Victorian father who wishes to be called Sir – he is a hands on dad, with an overflowing heart of love for each of his children. We can call Him "Abba" – the word that Jewish toddlers say all the time – it means "Daddy" 'For his Holy Spirit speaks to us deep within our hearts and tells us that we are God's children' (Romans 8:16 –NLT) In Hosea 11:1 there is a beautiful picture of God teaching His children to walk. Imagine God taking us by the hands, encouraging us to take our first wobbly steps, being there to catch us when we fall, being there to praise when we stand.

Not only do we have our Father God to hold our hand in this life, we have eternal life to enjoy in heaven with Him. After all, heaven is our Father's house (John 14:1) We have an inheritance kept for us there 'that can never perish, spoil or fade' (I Peter 1:4- NIV) As God's Word tells us- 'Now if we are children, then we are heirs – heirs of God and co-heirs with Christ' (Romans 8:17 – NIV) 'And since we are his children, we will share his treasures – for everything God gives to his Son, Christ, is ours, too'   (Romans 8:17 – NLT)

'How great is the love the Father has lavished on us, that we should be called children of God! And that is what we are!'   (I John 3:1 - NIV)

Father to child

Why are you so sad and troubled,
Discouraged and in a muddle?
Why do you try to cope on your own?
You don't have to do anything alone.
My child, come to me.
Stop struggling, I'll set you free.
My child, just ask.
My peace is within your grasp,
My arms are all around.
Seek me in prayer- I will be found.
I'm Your Father, Best Friend and though Lord of All,
I'm interested in you- things both great and small.
I want to share in your hopes and fears,
Be with you in joy, wipe away your tears.
So, why do you sink in cares and worry?
I'll take them from you, if you give them to me.
I am with you constantly,
You cannot run away from me.
No-one can snatch you out of my hand,
Safe and secure with me you stand.
Nothing can separate you from my love,
Nothing in earth or heaven above.
I love you because you re precious to me.
Stop struggling. Just stop. And trust in me

The love of God means
we are never alone

The Spirit, our comforter

Readings: Psalm 139:1-12, Psalm 121

Both our children are very attached to their "go-gos"-
their fleecy blankets that have been present since birth,
and must be there "to twiddle" as they go asleep! They
are a source of comfort and security- and life gets very
difficult when they can't be found! (Or when they need
to be washed!)

In John 14:16, Jesus promised a Comforter – the Holy
Spirit, to be with us forever. To be with us forever – let
that sink in – we are never alone! The Greek word is
parakletos – 'one coming to stand by you, one called
alongside to help'

When Caris was 4 she decided to start Irish dancing.
The class festival was just 4 weeks later. As I drove there,
I wondered how she was going to be brave enough to
dance on stage. I shouldn't have worried, for when it was
Caris' turn, one of the teenage dancers held her hand and
danced alongside her. It's a small picture of our Helper-
who holds our hand, keeps us going in the right direction, and dances through life with us.

God has promised – "Never will I leave you; never
will I forsake you."   (Hebrews 13:5 – NIV)

No matter where we go, God is there with us – wanting to reach out to us, wanting to love us, wanting to lead us on and help us through! 'Is there any place I can go to avoid your spirit? To be out of your sight? If I climb to the sky, you're there! If I go underground, you're there! If I flew on morning's wings to the far western horizon, you'd find me in a minute- you're already there waiting!'   (Psalm 139:7-11 – The Message)

No matter what we face, God is with us. God said to Joshua "Have I not commanded you? Be strong and courageous. Do not be terrified; do not be discouraged, for the Lord your God will be with you wherever you go."   (Joshua 1:9 – NIV)

> And Joshua faced the huge obstacle of the walls of Jericho.
> Just like Moses had the Red Sea looming in front.
> And David faced the giant Goliath.
> And Daniel was thrown into a lion's den.
> And Shadrach, Meshach and Abednego were thrown into the fiery furnace.
> And Elijah confronted the prophets of Baal.

Yet, they could all say with confidence, "The Lord is my helper, I will not be afraid" (Hebrews 13:6 – NIV) And we can say that too, for, we are never alone – we have God with us, every step of the way.

I love watching my children. The best time to watch them is when they are not aware that I am! I love watching them play, and use their vivid imaginations. I love listening to their chatter. But best of all, I love watching them sleep – so content, and unaware of my presence.

God is watching over us too – when we're not aware that He is even there! He watches over us night and day,

as we come and go. He's always there – and never
snoozes or sleeps.

We have His promise: "And surely I am with you
always, to the very end of the age"

(Matthew 28:20- NIV)

'You will lead the people you have redeemed with Your
faithful love'   (Exodus 15:13- HCSB)

'God is closer than you think!'

The love of God is boundless

The power of Your love

Reading: Romans 8:28-38

The love of God is overwhelming. It goes beyond dimensions of time and space. It is truly boundless and sacrificial. It means our past is forgiven, today is for really living, and our future is secure. Compared to this deep, agape love of God, all other loves pale into insignificance. And what is more, nothing can separate us from this love.

'And I am convinced that nothing can ever separate us from His love. Death can't, and life can't. The angels can't, and the demons can't. Our fears for today, our worries about tomorrow, and even the powers of hell can't keep God's love away. Whether we are high above the sky or in the deepest ocean, nothing in all creation will ever be able to separate us from the love of God that is revealed in Christ Jesus our Lord'

(Romans 8:38 &39 – NLT)

'Paul looks round all created worlds – he looks at the might of the mightiest archangel – the satanic power of legions of devils – the united forces of all created things; and when he sees sinners folded in the arms of Jesus, he cries, "Who shall separate us from the love of Christ?" not all the forces of ten thousand worlds combined, for Jesus is greater than all. 'We are more than conquerors though him that loved us'

'The love of Christ! Paul says: "The love of Christ passes knowledge" It is like the blue sky into which you may see clearly, but the real vastness of which you cannot measure. It is like the deep, deep sea into which you can look a little way, but its depths are unfathomable' (Robert Murray M'Cheyne)[6]

'Your unfailing love, O Lord, is as vast as the heavens; your faithfulness reaches beyond the clouds'

(Psalm 36:6-NLT)

This love should make our heart sing and our spirit soar!

God is love. God **is** love! God is **love**!

The very essence of God is love. At the heart of God…is love.

'May the Lord bring you into an ever deeper understanding of the love of God'

(II Thessalonians 3:5 – NLT)

'May the Lord direct your hearts into God's love'

(II Thessalonians 3:5 – NIV)

True love:

For God so loVed the world
   That He gave
     His Only Son
   That whoever believes
        In Him
    Shall not
       Die but have
     Eternal
     Life
John 3:16
God is love!

God is love!

'God gave us life-Jesus gave us eternity'

'And so we know and rely on the love God has for us. God is love' (I John 4:16 – NIV)

Thank You God!

Lord, I thank You for Your amazing, unending, unquenchable love:

- A love that cost your Son His life.
- A love that began in eternity past.
- A love that forgives my sin – my failures and shortcomings.
- A love that redeems and restores.
- A love that forgets the past.
- A love that brings joy to the present.
- A love that brings hope to the future.
- A love that has adopted me into Your family.
- A love that gives life purpose and direction.
- A love that has no limits.
- A love that knows no barriers.
- A love that stretches beyond our farthest horizons.
- A love that reached down to me, just where I was.
- A love that has done more than we could ever dare to imagine.

- A love that can only come from
  You – my awesome Father God.

I thank You from the bottom of my heart.
I thank You with all that I am.
I thank You with all that I've got.

I thank You for this love You've poured unreservedly into my life:

- A love I don't deserve
- A love I could never earn.
- A love I can never fully comprehend.
- A love that is mine to embrace and enjoy.
- A love that is Your gift to me – Your gift of grace.

Thank You God - I want to say thank You with my life.

PART 2

LOVING GOD

'Love the Lord your God with all your heart and
with all your soul and with all your strength'
(Deuteronomy 6:5 – NIV)

'Love God, your God, with your whole heart: love Him
with all that's in you; love Him with all you've got!'
(Deuteronomy 6:5 – The Message)

Loving God means knowing His Name

What's in a name?

Readings: Psalm 9, Exodus 3

There are many books on the shelves in bookshops and many sites on the web to help you choose baby names. You will find both traditional and modern names, Irish and Biblical names, common and unusual names. For as parents, we have the daunting task of choosing names for our children – names that they will be known by for all of their lives. Romantics like Rob and I chose the names of our children while we were dating! Our daughter is called Caris Katrina – Caris from the Greek word Charis, which means grace, and Katrina after beautiful Loch Katrine in the Trossachs. Our son was named Ethan Ben – Ethan meaning 'strong and steadfast' after the renowned musician in charge of music in the tabernacle and writer of Psalm 89. He even played the cymbals when the ark was brought to Jerusalem! (I Chronicles 15:17-19) Ben means 'favoured of God' and is also the Gaelic word for mountain (Ben Aan is our favourite!)

If the meaning of the names of our children is important, how much more important it is to know our God's Name and the meaning behind it! For, 'Those who know your name will trust you, for you, Lord, have never forsaken those who seek you' (Psalm 9:10 – NIV)

The Lord appeared to Abram and said, "I am God Almighty" (Genesis 17:1 – NIV) Our God is El Shaddai – the All Powerful One. He was strong enough to set the planets into orbit, and He is strong enough to carry our burdens – and strong enough to carry us! In Genesis 22, Abraham learnt from difficult testing that God's Name is also Jehovah Jireh ('The Lord will provide') God who provided a ram for Abraham at just the right time, who provided a Saviour for our fallen world at just the right time, will provide for our needs too. 'And my God will meet all your needs according to his glorious riches in Christ Jesus' (Philippians 4:19 –NIV) - whatever we need. In Genesis 16:13, Hagar, Abraham's servant girl, referred to God as El Roi-'the God who sees me' He sees us when we try to run and hide. He sees our personal lives-who we are when no one (else) is looking- and He still loves us!

Moses stood barefoot on holy ground before the burning bush, and asked God His Name. God replied "Yahweh" (Exodus 3:14). Yahweh is derived from the Hebrew word for "I am" – God is saying "I am who I am", "I will be what I will be" and "I am the one who always is" He is eternal and unchanging. Only our God can say, "There never was a time when I was not. There will never be a time when I will not be." We can totally depend on our great, unchangeable God in our very changeable world.

In Exodus 15:22-27, the Israelites were thirsty, yet found only bitter water at Marah. God made the water sweet and used it as an object lesson to reveal His Name – Yahweh Rapha – "I am The Lord, who heals you" (Ex

15:26 –NIV) Our God can heal our hurts, our disappointments and our illnesses. He can make life's bitter moments sweet.

Just a little further on in Exodus 17:8-16, the Israelites were fighting the Amalekites, and they won as long as Moses' hands were raised in prayer. The banner of victory was flown, and Moses built an altar as a symbol of God's Name – Jehovah Nissi –'The Lord is my banner'. The Lord is our Strong Deliverer. He will lead us into victory in the battles we face, and often the real battlefield is at the place of prayer.

Years later, at the time of the judges, when the Israelites had been given over to the Midianites, God revealed another facet of His character to His hero Gideon – Yahweh Shalom –'The Lord is peace' (Judges 6:24) In the midst of conflict, Gideon knew the peace of God, for he knew the God of peace. We too can know God's shalom peace in the storms of life.

God's Name is a place we can run to. Our Father's arms are open wide, to comfort and protect. For, 'The name of the Lord is a strong tower; the righteous run to it and are safe.'   (Proverbs 18:10-NIV)

Loving God means knowing Jesus

Like Father, like Son

Reading: John 6

How often we see family resemblances between fathers and sons. Often they have the same mannerisms and facial expressions, the same sayings and ways of doing things! The family likeness exists to a much deeper extent than we will ever be able to comprehend between God the Father and His Son Jesus. For, 'The Son is the radiance of God's glory and the exact representation of his being' (Hebrews 1:3 –NIV) Jesus is totally, unquestionably God, yet for our sake He left heaven, propelled by love, and became truly man on earth. 'The word became flesh and blood, and moved into the neighbourhood. We saw the glory with our own eyes, the one-of-a-kind glory, like Father, like Son'

(John 1:14 –The Message)

When on earth, Jesus caused outrage by claiming He was God. He stated "I tell you the truth, before Abraham was born, I am" (John 8:58 -NIV) This is a very powerful statement. By saying He existed before Abraham, He proclaimed His divinity, and He also applied God's holy Name, I am, to Himself.

If we love God, we must love his Son, Jesus as our Lord and Saviour.

After feeding 5000 people, with two fish and five loaves of bread, Jesus said: "I am the bread of life" (John 6: 35 –NIV) He is the One who not only supplies our daily bread, but also gives spiritual nourishment and eternal satisfaction.

Jesus also proclaimed, "I am the light of the world" (John 8: 12 –NIV) He shines in the darkness of hard times and shows up the path through life to stop us stumbling along the way.

Jesus said, "I am the gate; whoever enters through me will be saved." (John 10:9 – NIV) He is the wide open door to God. 'We have peace with God through our Lord Jesus Christ, through whom we have gained access by faith into this grace in which we now stand'

(Rom 5: 1&2 – NIV)

Later in the same chapter, Jesus said, "I am the good shepherd" (John 10:11– NIV) We can know the tender watch-care of the Lord, our Shepherd. 'Like a shepherd, he will care for his flock, gathering the lambs in his arms, hugging them as he carries them' (Isaiah 40:11 – The Message) At our Friday morning Bible study, we discovered this great promise for mums: 'He gently leads those that have young.'   (Isaiah 40:11 –NIV)

At the grave of His friend Lazarus, He said, "I am the resurrection and the life. He who believes in me will live, even though he dies" (John 11:25 –NIV) Because He lives, death is not the end. We have the sure and certain hope of heaven and eternal life.

After talking about heaven, Jesus proclaimed, "I am the way, the truth and the life" (John 14:6 –NIV) He is the way (the only way) to our Father's House, the absolute truth and the essence of true, fulfilling, never-ending life itself.

In the last of the seven (the number of perfection) 'I am' sayings, Jesus said, "I am the true vine" He is the source of fruitfulness. We must remain in Him, for apart from him we can do nothing   (John 15:5)

If we have Jesus, we have the greatest treasure that man can ever find. For, if we know Jesus as our Saviour, we have nourishment to sustain us. We have Light in the darkness, access to the Father, a Shepherd to carry us, eternal Life, absolute Truth and the Source of fruitfulness.

'I am the good shepherd; I know my own sheep, and they know me, just as my Father knows me and I know the Father. And I lay down my life for the sheep'

(John 10:14&15 – NLT)

Loving God means spending time with Him

Take a break!

Reading: Psalm 46

Life today moves at a hectic pace. We rush from one appointment to the next- ticking off our "to do" list as we go, meeting deadlines, sending text messages on our mobile phones en route! We can use our laptops or palm tops on the journey, then there's the e-mails to deal with and "snail mail" and junk mail when we get home! We seem to spend all our energy just about surviving. We barely have time to lift our heads. God is squeezed out of our daily routine.

> Lord, I've felt the emptiness
> Of days spent without You,
> Of time so "filled" with other things,
> That I don't have time for You.

In the middle of our rush and busyness, what is God trying to say? If we can hear His voice in our hectic schedule, He says, "Be still" (Psalm 46:10) – or as the Message puts it- "Step out of the traffic!" Get off the motorway, onto the B road, the scenic route, the road less travelled. Stop and look around! Smell the roses! Watch the sunset! Gaze at the stars! Kick some leaves! Have a mellow coffee with a friend! Take the kids to the beach! Seize the day! Celebrate the moment! This is your life- not a dress rehearsal! No-one is going to get to the end of their life and wish that they had sent more e-mails, attended more meetings, made more phone calls. So, take a deep breath and slow down– don't let what seems urgent rob you of what is really important.

God says, "Be still and know that I am God". The most important thing each day is to come to our God, to hear His voice. He says, "Come to Me, all you who are weary and burdened and I will give you rest" (Matthew 11:28- NIV). The next two verses in the Message say this – "Learn the unforced rhythms of grace. I won't lay anything heavy or ill-fitting on you. Keep company with me and you'll learn to live freely and lightly". We must slow down, get rid of distractions, clear away the clutter in our minds, banish to do lists. Sometimes we've got to leave what is good and choose what is better – quality time with God. Life goes better if we speak to Him before we speak to others. If our relationship with Him is first priority, all other relationships go more smoothly. Time with God is always the best option. Without Him we're just running on empty, getting stressed out and heading for burn out.

Each day God wants to guide us to make full use of limited time-not so we'll get dizzy with to-do lists-but so His priorities will be ours and we'll achieve what he wants - things that'll last.

When life seems busiest, we often need to stop and simply draw aside and come to our Heavenly Father, who knows what we really need. And sometimes our deepest need is to simply be still, to care for our soul and to find rest in God alone   (Psalm 62:1)

The Psalms are punctuated by the word 'Selah', or 'Interlude' as the Message translates it. We need to punctuate our life with interludes, quiet pauses with God.

'Step out of the traffic! Take a long, loving look at Me, your High God above everything'
                                    (Psalm 46:10 - The Message)

In the middle of busy days,
God give me quiet moments-
To pause and pray.
In the hectic busyness of life,
help me to be still.
To cease striving.
To calm down.
To catch my breath.

To forget about what's going on all around, cramming in on my mind.
Help me to be still, and know that You are God.
That You are in control

- when things are all right
- when things are all wrong
- when the pressure seems high
- when life tumbles down.

Even then and even now help me to be still and focus on You, rather than my problems.

Amen

'God, my shepherd!
I don't need a thing.
You have bedded me down in lush meadows,
You find me quiet pools to drink from.
True to your word,
You let me catch my breath
And send me in the right direction'

(Psalm 23:1-3-The Message)

Loving God means choosing what is best

The better thing

Reading: Luke 10:38-42

Imagine having at least 13 guests for dinner! Of course we can identify with Martha being flustered and distracted! There'd be so much to do – vegetables to prepare, tables to set, rooms to tidy, meat to roast. Of course we'd be annoyed if our sister wasn't helping! The Bible says that Mary was sitting at Jesus' feet, hanging on every word! In exasperation Martha asked Jesus to tell her sister to help. "Martha, Martha," the Lord answered, "you are worried and upset about many things, but only one thing is needed. Mary has chosen what is better and it will not be taken away from her" (Luke 10: 41&42-NIV)

Despite all the preparations for dinner, there was really only one thing worth being concerned about. Mary had left what was good to do and had chosen something better – God's best - spending unhurried quality time with Him.

And today, in the middle of our busy schedules, we daily face the same choice. Are we frazzled and distracted like Martha, or are we quietly content like Mary, resting in our Lord's presence? Often we too have to leave what is good, and choose what is better.

We may have to leave the dishes. Forget about the ironing (Not a problem for many of us!) Banish to do lists. Turn off the TV. Disconnect the phone. Shut the door. And climb into 'the closet' and sit at Jesus' feet- to hear what He has to say, to allow Him access to our hearts, to seek His face and His leading. There'll always be other things to do, but He should be our first priority.

We, like the psalmist, must yearn to grow as close to God as possible. 'One thing I ask of the Lord, this is what I seek; that I may dwell in the house of the Lord all the days of my life, to gaze upon the beauty of the lord and to seek him in his temple.' (Psalm 27:4 -NIV) 'O God, you are my God, earnestly I seek you'

(Psalm 63:1 –NIV)

We must get pleasure from being in God's presence. 'Delight yourself in the Lord and he will give you the desires of you heart' (Psalm 37:4 – NIV) 'You will seek me and find me when you seek me with all your heart' (Jeremiah 29:13 –NIV) When we spend quality time with God, our reward is God Himself.

'Sow for yourselves righteousness, reap the fruit of unfailing love, and break up your unploughed ground, for it is time to seek the Lord, until he comes and showers righteousness on you' (Hosea 10:12 –NIV) We need to ask God to soften our hearts, to plough up the hard areas so that we can be teachable and re- sponsive to His voice. If we seek the Lord, He will shower blessings on us. If we, like Mary, leave what is good and choose what is better, we too will receive God's best.

'Draw close to God, and God will draw close to you'
(James 4:8 –NLT)

Father, You **are** the best- better than everything else!

May I get to know You more, for it is in first seeking Your face that I can face everything else. May I do those good works you've planned for me to do. May I accomplish what You want. May I fulfil Your agenda rather than my own and reach my maximum potential in You.

Loving God means living for Him daily

The will of God

Readings: Matthew 6:33& 34, Psalm 32:8

Someone once said, "The will of God is a bigger thing than you bargain for" – and it is, but sometimes it's about little things – regular everyday stuff. There's a danger in making discovering God's will into some huge, mysterious lifetime quest. By doing so, we overlook how practical it is. God wants us to discover His will for our lives on a daily basis. The apostle Paul asked that God would fill the church with the knowledge of His will 'in order that you may live a life worthy of the Lord and may please Him in every way bearing fruit in every good work, growing in the knowledge of God.'   (Colossians 1:9 & 10 – NIV)

We should pray that God would reveal what He wants to do specifically – each day, for the future comes one day at a time. Simply asking our Father at the start of each day "What do you want me to accomplish today? Help me to do it" makes every day an adventure with God. There's great liberty and release from pressure. God's agenda becomes our agenda. We become more concerned with God's heart rather than merely ticking off to do lists. We commit our daily lives to Him and become aware of God given opportunities. We grasp that each day has eternal potential, and that by doing what God wants, rather than what we want that we can make an everlasting difference to those around us.

For it's the daily things that mount up – that go to make a lifetime. We don't want to miss the point by waiting on some big step God wants us to take, when little ones will take us in the right direction. We don't want to stay in the rock pools 'playing' at Christianity, when God wants us to 'launch out' into the deep water and feel the exhilaration of truly following Him – through the swell, the highs and lows, even the storms, to the calm on the other side!

We don't want to just be working towards a bigger house, a newer car and gaining more and more things to make our comfort zone more and more comfortable, when there's a world out there literally dying to know our God. There are jobs that God has planned for us to do in eternity past that only we can do (not because we are great but because He is!) that will have a lasting effect on eternity in the future.

Therefore 'Steep your life in God-reality, God initiative, God-provisions. Don't worry about missing out. You'll find your everyday human concerns will be met.

Give your entire attention to what God is doing right now, and don't get worked up about what may or may not happen tomorrow. God will help you deal with whatever hard things come up when the time comes'

(Matthew 6:33,34 The Message)

Father God,
    I want to live for You – to bring a smile to Your face and joy to Your heart.

'The will of God- nothing more, nothing less, nothing else!'

Loving God means loving His Word

Milkaholics and chocoholics!

Readings: Hebrews 5:11-6:1, Psalm 19:7-11

Newborn babies just love to guzzle their milk – they really are milkaholics! It's no surprise that Paul chose to use them as an object lesson when he wrote 'like newborn babies crave pure spiritual milk so that by it you may grow up in your salvation' (I Peter 2:2-NIV) I wonder what we crave, what we truly desire. We must drink deep from God's Word, our spiritual milk so that we will nourish our soul and grow 'big and strong' in the Lord. All mothers are concerned that their babies are taking adequate amounts of milk to thrive and gain weight. And God is no different – He wants us to grow in our faith by feeding on His Word.

Of course, babies feed on milk alone for a relatively short time. At the magical age of 16 weeks (sorry 6 months by latest guidelines!), weaning begins! And the mega-efficient mums have home prepared purees at the ready, while the more unorganised among us reach for the tins of baby food (organic, of course – to ease our conscience!) One week it's baby rice on the menu, the next pureed carrot is introduced (and their little bibs have indelible orange stains!) Before you know it, they're having mashed broccoli, banana and apple and blueberry! Their little taste buds are experiencing new delights everyday, and the baby rice is too bland to tempt them!

In our spiritual growth, we too must take the step from milk to solid food (I Corinthians 3:2) We mustn't fall into the trap of going over the basics again, and again – but rather become mature in our understanding
(Hebrews 5:11-6:1)

Our babies soon become toddlers – and we try to encourage a balanced diet – and try not to get frustrated with their food fads and picky eating! We too need a balanced spiritual diet- the carbohydrate of Paul's teachings, the protein of God's Word through Moses, the essential fatty acids of the Gospels, the refreshing fruit of Psalms and Proverbs, the vitamins of prophecy, the balance of history contained in both the Old and New Testaments.

If babies are milkaholics, many of their mums are chocoholics! (I've just eaten some delicious Cadbury's mini eggs – and it's nowhere near Easter!) There's no doubt, chocolate certainly has a feel good factor, as it releases endorphins in our bodies. Indeed, whole books have been written on the positive effects of chocolate! But it's so more-ish, and if we're not careful, we'll soon be piling on the pounds! We certainly can't survive physically on junk food alone, yet many of us try to spiritually. We snack on God's Word – we read a quick verse here and there, have a little 'thought for the day' when we get a chance. And by doing so, we miss out on the deeply satisfying and refreshing experience of feasting on God's Word, of hearing what He has to say to us. When we take time to properly digest God's Word, and meditate on it, it will affect our spiritual bodies. 'Through the Word we are put together and shaped up for the tasks God has for us' (II Timothy 3:17-The Message)

'People need more than bread for their life, they must feed on every word of God' (Matthew 4:4-NLT) Just as the Israelites gathered manna daily, so we must gather from God's Word – the nourishment for our souls each day. Being well fed yesterday, doesn't take away our hunger pangs today!

God's Word should be our delight and we should meditate on its truth (Psalm 1:2) Meditating literally means mulling it over- like a cow chewing cud! This means God's Word will go down deep- penetrating the core of our being. Daily nourishment slowly, consistently transforms our thoughts and ultimately our lives.

After all, God's Word is powerful- sharper than a two edged sword in our hand, sharper than a surgeon's scalpel. It is a lamp to guide our feet- to show life's path. It is living and active- it's dynamic. It is God-breathed. It is God's instruction book to us, a love letter to His people.

It is the Bread of Life and Living Water. It is the food that we can't keep to ourselves-but have to share with others.

At times we may lose our appetite for spiritual food- but these are the very times that we need it. We must force ourselves to read, knowing that it will do us good even if we don't enjoy the experience at that particular time.

So, no matter what, let's make time to read and study God's Word, our Precious Book, today and everyday from now on.

'Your word is a lamp for my feet and a light for my path' (Psalm 119:105-NIV)

Loving God means relying on Him

Me do it myself!

Reading: Philippians 4:10-23

"Me do it myself!" Caris said. Not realising just how determined she was, I tried to help a little. "NO!! Me do it myself!" she shouted even louder. And I was forced just to watch while my little toddler tried and struggled and tried and squirmed to get her trousers on all by herself!

You may be smiling as you remember your own little toddler's similar struggles. Yet, how often we have just the same toddler attitude with God. He is there wanting to help us, but we're determined to do it all by ourselves. And we might even throw a tantrum or two when things don't work out as we'd anticipated. And we carry on struggling and struggling with our baggage and burdens, reluctant to hand it all over to our Father God. He stands watching in the background and waiting. Waiting for the moment when we ask Him to carry the load with us, when we hand it over and rely on Him.

With all the resources of heaven available to us, why do we keep insisting on going it alone?

The little wristband 'F.R.O.G.' reminds us of how we should be- Fully Relying On God.

And Jesus said, "Apart from me you can do nothing."
(John 15:5- NIV)
We are nothing without Him.

We are like:

- A ship without a sail
- An eagle without wings
- A door without a key
- A letter without words
- A glove without a hand

Yet, if we're nothing without Him, with Him we are everything.

HIS strength is at work within us. God's mighty power is available to us (Ephesians 1:19) His stone-moving, death-defeating, life-giving power! The Greek word for power used here literally means dynamite!

Paul wrote, 'For I can do everything with the help of Christ who gives me the strength I need' (Philippians 4:13-NLT) 'Whatever I have, wherever I am, I can make it through anything in the One who makes me who I am'
(Philippians 4:13-The Message)

His power is all around-we just need to get plugged in!!

But that's the trouble- so often we're not. We're still trying to do it all –alone. Often it's a simple matter-'You do not have, because you do not ask God'
(James 4:2-NIV)

Once upon a time, a man had a dream. St. Peter was giving him a tour of heaven. Just beyond the golden streets, there were huge barns everywhere. The man was curious and asked, "What's inside the barns?" "They are full of boxes of blessings that God has ready for each of

His children, but they've never asked for!" replied St. Peter.

We need to ask, for He is ready to give.

'I have strength for all things in Christ Who empowers me (I am ready for anything and equal to anything through Him Who infuses inner strength into me; I am self-sufficient in Christ's sufficiency)'

(Philippians 4:13- AMP)

It is enough to simply ask the Father!

He giveth more grace

He giveth more grace when the burdens grow greater,
He sendeth more strength when the labours increase;
To added affliction He addeth His mercies,
To multiplied trials His multiplied peace.

When we have exhausted our store of endurance,
When our strength has failed ere the day is half done,
When we reach the end of our hoarded resources
Our Father's full giving is only begun.

His love has no limit, His grace has no measure,
His power no boundary known unto men;
For out of His infinite riches in Jesus
He giveth and giveth and giveth again.

(Annie Johnson Flint)

Loving God means keeping our love alive

Remembering our first love

Readings: Revelation 2:1-7 & 3:14-22

I'm sure you remember well those incredible early feelings of being in love- the butterflies, loss of appetite, lack of sleep, silly grins and general giddiness! Of course those initial feelings can't last forever – they give way to something just as special, but much deeper.

When Rob and I were going out, some of our most special times were spent on day hikes –in the Mournes, or Glen Clova and Glencoe in Scotland. We were able to escape from everyday pressures and distractions, enjoy God's creation and just spend quality time talking to each other for hours! Of course, now, 9 1/2 years and 2 children later, it's been a very long time since we went on a day hike! But we were just saying last night that this summer we'd have to schedule a day hike – just the two of us!

In every marriage, we have to work at keeping the love alive. It takes time and effort. It's the same with our relationship with God. There's a honeymoon period after we become a Christian – an incredible closeness to God. We are captivated by God's love. And as we go through life with God, we must remain, or abide in God's love (John 15:4) We can do this by having a conscious awareness of His presence with us. We can consult Him about things that affect us. We should continue to enjoy Him as a Person.

Of course, all this requires spending time with our Father God. What would our marriages be like if we spoke to our husbands as little as we speak to God?

Our relationship with God can deteriorate into something quite mundane and cold, if we're not careful. The church at Ephesus was rebuked for this very reason: "Yet this I hold against you. You have forsaken your first love. Repent and do the things you did at first"

(Revelation 2:4 – NIV)

"Backslider" is a very emotive word. But, if we've ever been closer to God than we are now, then surely we've "backslidden" In our journey through life with God, we don't stay static. We either move forward with purpose, or else we drift- and the drifting tends to be backward.

'To everyman there openeth
A way and ways and a way.
And the high soul climbs the high way
And the low soul gropes the low
And in between on the misty flats
The rest drift to and fro.
But to everyman there openeth
A high way and a low
And everyman decideth the way
His soul should go'

(John Oxenham)

It's all about choices- we choose which way our relationship with God goes – whether we're walking closely to Him, or far away. We decide if we're going to make our relationship with God our first priority- if we're going to go the highway and enjoy real intimacy with our God.

Just as we make daily choices that affect the quality of our marriage, so it is with our relationship with God. We may have started off well, with fervour, loving being in love with God. But now, much worse than being cold, we're lukewarm – as stagnant as tepid water. We're ambivalent, indifferent, and mediocre. We're in between on the misty flats drifting to and fro.

Many of us are prodigals. Of course, we're still our Father's children – nothing can change that. But we're certainly not close to our Father- we're living in a distant land, far from the Father's house. We've squandered His riches, freely given to us. We're missing out on the privileges of His children – we're searching for scraps in the pigsty when we could be feasting at His table.

Maybe today, we need to come home, to return to our Father's house, to feel the warmth of His embrace and the unspeakable joy of a restored relationship. There'll be no anger, or awkward questions, just His tender voice saying, "Welcome home" and His deep unconditional love- the love that He's been aching to show us while we were apart. And we'll wonder why we were away so long – away from our Father's house, but we'll realise that we were never, never away from our Father's love.

'Delight yourself in the Lord and he will give you the desires of your heart'   (Psalm 37:4 – NIV)

Loving God means learning to love ourselves

Inner beauty

Readings: I Peter 3:3&4, Romans 5:1-5

Many of us struggle with low self-esteem and poor self-confidence. We are preoccupied with our flaws and physical imperfections. We gaze in the mirror and see our big nose, crooked teeth, extra pounds, knobbly knees and those bags under our eyes! And it's not just our physical pitfalls that we dwell on – we've got emotional hang-ups and intellectual shortcomings too. We're hard on ourselves, and find it hard to accept compliments.

Too often, we're so busy navel gazing that we don't grasp our true worth in God's eyes. We find it difficult to accept His love, and we therefore lack confidence to reach out to others with His love. If we don't love ourselves, we'll find it nearly impossible to love others.

Both my children were born with birthmarks in the middle of their foreheads. When an Asian paediatrician came to do Ethan's baby check when he was just 3 days old, he exclaimed that if my children had been born in his Hindu culture, the whole village would have came to see them! For, the mark on their forehead meant that they had been blessed by God!

I believe that we **are** truly blessed by our God! We are 'blessed out of our boots!' as our friend Billy O'Mahony once exclaimed!

God has poured his love into our hearts and:

- we have been justified through faith   (Romans 5:1)
- we have peace with God   (Romans 5:1)
- we have access by faith 'into the wide open spaces of God's grace and glory'   (Romans 5:2- The Message)
- we rejoice in our sufferings   (Romans 5:3)
- we have been chosen before time
- we are set apart for eternity
- we have been redeemed by Jesus' precious blood
- we are called to be holy
- we have been promised an inheritance in heaven
- we are secure in God's hands

Rick Warren wrote these five purposes for life, in his book The Purpose Driven Life[1]:

(1) You were planned for God's Pleasure
(2) You were formed for God's Family
(3) You were created to become like Christ
(4) You were shaped for serving God
(5) You were made for a mission

We have everlasting significance, and eternal value. We have purpose in life.

We **are** all blessed by God- we have been marked out to be different. We are unique from everyone else! We have our own distinctive temperament, gifts, background, insights, interests & ideas! We are His workmanship (Ephesians 2:10) – literally His masterpiece, His work of art. We are His children, bought at a great price. We are made in His image – and we are beautiful in His eyes.

God looks beyond our outward appearance, and straight to our heart. It's not our clothes, our jewellery or our hair that catches our Maker's attention! It's inner beauty – 'the unfading beauty of a gentle and quiet spirit' (I Peter 3:4 –NIV) He wants us to concentrate on what is really important, to learn to love ourselves, to see ourselves the way He does.

"Don't be afraid," he said, for you are deeply loved by God. Be at peace; take heart and be strong!'

(Daniel 10:19-NLT)

Because of Him, we can feel loved. We are loved. We are deeply loved by God. We can walk tall and hold our head high. We are after all, daughters of the King of kings.

Of course we'll mess up, fall down and let ourselves (and God) down from time to time, but don't loose heart- the treasure is in earthen vessels, jars of clay but G. I. F. W. U. Y. - God isn't finished with us yet!

He looks beyond our weakness to our potential. In fact He chooses the weak to shame the strong (I Corinthians 1:27) We are clay in the hands of the Potter. We are the canvas on which the Great Artist is creating a masterpiece with His brushstrokes. We are work in progress and the end result won't be seen this side of eternity.

But, today and every day, we can be assured that God loves us - and we should therefore love ourselves!

'My song is love unknown,
My Saviour's love for me

59

Love to the loveless shown,
That they might lovely be'

(Samuel Crossman 1624-1683)

'If God had a refrigerator, your picture would be on it.
If He had a wallet, your photo would be in it.
He sends you flowers every spring
and a sunrise every morning.
Whenever you want to talk, he'll listen.
He can live anywhere in the universe,
and he chose your heart.
And the Christmas gift he sent you in Bethlehem?
Face it, friend. He's crazy about you'

(Max Lucado)[2]

> *'You're the apple of his eye,*
> *And the delight of His heart'*

Loving God means
valuing what He has given

The thing about things!

Reading: Ephesians 1:3-14

Today, it seems like the main thing is to accumulate more and more things! There are things everywhere – in shops, on line, in catalogues and on television. Retail therapy has become a major past time. There are just so many must-have, gotta-get items, gadgets and gizmos. It has reached the stage where we love things and use people rather than the other way round.

But really, the best things in life aren't things! They are the things that money can't buy. You can't put a price on a loving husband, a beautiful baby, a supportive family or good health. God 'richly provides us with everything for our enjoyment' (I Timothy 6:17- NIV) He has provided all that we need and much, much more. His Word says 'A life devoted to things is a dead life, a stump; a God-shaped life is a flourishing tree' (Proverbs 11:28- The Message) 'A simple life in the Fear-of-God is better than a rich life with a ton of headaches.'

(Proverbs 15:16- The Message)

We have been given every spiritual blessing – the riches of God's grace have been lavished on us

(Ephesians 1:3,7&8) As Pastor Baird quoted in a sermon last year, "We have been given the treasure of knowing God, the gold of His grace, the rich jewel of redeeming love and the everlasting resources of His Kingdom"

How does God want us to respond to His extravagant provision for us? 'Command them to do good, to be rich in good deeds, and to be generous and willing to share. In this way they will lay up treasure for themselves as a firm foundation for the coming age, so that they may take hold of life that is truly life'

(I Timothy 6:18 – NIV)

We need to be thankful for the good things that we've got! 'Enjoy what you have rather than desiring what you don't have' (Ecclesiastes 6:9-NLT)

Enjoy the gifts and live a life of thankfulness to the Giver!

"He who is richest is rich in God's love"

Loving God means getting rid of what hinders

Excess baggage!

Readings: Hebrews 12:1&2, Romans 12:1&2

They say that you can tell a lot about someone by the contents of their handbag! I'm just not sure what the psychoanalysts would make of the average mum's bag! There'd be an eclectic assortment of dummies, wipes (both used and unused!), post-its with scribbled 'to-do lists', a nappy or two, letters to post, and a half used lipstick!

All mothers have the huge task of assembling 'the bag' to take to hospital with them prior to giving birth. And all the pregnancy magazines compile lists of the absolute essentials to bring – for both mother and baby! Then, after our little darlings arrive, we spend the next 3 years carting another bag around with us! A bag with solutions for every mishap and requirements for every need- nappies, wipes, complete change of clothes, snacks, juice, toys and books!

I don't know if you've ever been accused of having excess baggage when travelling. One time that sticks in my mind was as a student travelling to Dundee. I had a large rucksack on my back, a slightly smaller one on my front, and a sports bag in each hand!! (I also know some-one who managed to get an entire Denby dinner set on as hand luggage on a transatlantic flight!!)

Last year, for an extra challenge, a man did the London marathon in flippers and diving suit. He arrived at the finish line a few days after the other competitors had finished! How much easier it would have been if he had got rid of the excess baggage and ran in shorts and T-shirt!

Today, many of us are burdened with excess baggage. Old regrets, past hurts and current fears weigh us down. God's Word tells us to 'strip off every weight that slows us down, especially the sin that so easily hinders our progress' (Hebrews 12:1-NLT) We are commanded to 'get rid of all bitterness, rage and anger, brawling and slander, along with every form of malice'

(Ephesians 4:32-NIV)

I'm sure many of you are familiar with the story Pilgrim's Progress. There's one part where pilgrims burden rolls down the hill at the cross. Yet how many of us pick up the very burdens that Jesus died to free us from!

Paul urges us 'Do not conform any longer to the pattern of this world, but be transformed by the renew-ing of your mind' (Romans 12:2-NIV) We are not to be conformed or squeezed into the world's mould, but rather transformed. The word here is literally metamorphosis-we are transformed from a lowly caterpillar, bound to the earth into a graceful butterfly, soaring the heights above!

Loving God means having His perspective

The big picture!

Readings: II Corinthians 4:16-18, Isaiah 40:27-31

There are some good days, a lot of average days, and some days (including Mondays and bad hair days!) that just totally convince you that Murphy's Law is alive and active and still holds true!

If something can go wrong, it will! The toast will land buttered side down on the floor. You will sleep in on a day you REALLY have to get to work early (and you'll get stuck in a traffic jam en route!) It won't just rain- it'll pour. And it'll pour even harder if you've organised a barbeque! The children will misbehave in front of VIPs (The more important the visitor, the worse the behaviour!) Every single one of the toys you tidied up will be tipped back out and scattered to the four corners of the room as soon as your back is turned!

You will forget the very thing that you were trying desperately hard to remember. The dinner will get burnt when there are guests there to eat it. The milk will get spilt, and there really isn't any point crying over it! The Denby from your wedding list will get broke- and so will your heart. The brand-new pretty pink dress will get covered in mud (or worse!) the very first time your little darling wears it- and the washing powder won't do half as much as the advert claimed it would! You will find the thing you lost as soon as you replace it.

Oh, there may be a few perfect days-or nearly perfect ones anyhow! Days when life is how we want it to be, when we feel shiny and happy. Days when everything goes according to plan- without hitches or hiccoughs. But often, days will quickly go pear-shaped, and our days will have unexpected twists and not turn out quite as we anticipated.

The sort of 'bad days' described above, aren't really too bad in the grand scheme of things. But we will all go through truly difficult days. Our life can be altered forever by a phone call. A diagnosis can change life's course. An accident, a break up, a failure, or disappointments can make it seem like the bottom has fallen out of our world and we're free falling. And we don't know where we'll end up-or in what shape!

In all these things, we need to have God's perspective. 'For our present troubles are quite small and won't last very long. Yet they produce for us an immeasurably great glory that will last forever!' (II Corinthians 4:17-NLT)

When troubles come, eagles stretch their wings and fly into the sky, knowing that the storm will carry it higher than it could soar on its own. Yet, how often we're more like ostriches! We bury our heads in the sand, and don't surface until we think the storm has gone away!

An old poem says:
'Two prisoners in jail, behind bars.
One looked down and saw mud.
The other looked up and saw stars'

Often, we too can't see the stars, because we're staring down at the mud. Our glass is always half empty, rather than half full. (And often we're so contrary that we're thinking, "I didn't even order this drink anyhow!")

In Numbers 13, the spies reported on their exploration of the Promised Land. It truly was a land flowing with milk and honey, containing huge fruit. But most of the spies just couldn't see past the giants who lived there in fortified cities. They left God out of the equation. And often- we're the same- we can't see beyond the giants looming in our mind to God Himself.

We need to have God's perspective – the bigger picture. We need to see things from His viewpoint. 'Let the beloved of the Lord rest secure in him, for he shields him all day long, and the one the Lord loves rests between his shoulders.' (Deuteronomy 33:12-NIV) And when we are resting on God Almighty's shoulders, the giants will shrink, and not seem quite so giant anymore!

'So we don't look at the troubles we can see right now; rather, we look forward to what we have not yet seen. For the troubles we see will soon be over, but the joys to come will last forever.'   (II Corinthians 4:18-NLT)

When life sends rain, God sends rainbows!

Loving God means trusting Him each day

Don't worry about a thing

Readings: Matthew 6:25-34, Philippians 4:6&7

"Don't worry about a thing, 'cos every little thing's gonna be all right!" the popular song goes! It's easy to sing and easy to say but so much more difficult to do! Jesus said, "Do not worry" (Matthew 6:31) It's not a suggestion. It's a command. Yet how many of us know the stomach-churning, heart-thumping feeling of anxiety? Worrying distracts us, robs us of sleep, steals our joy and ruins the present moment.

In the days before Caris was born, I had a lot to worry about– getting to the hospital on time and knowing what to do, never mind the daunting prospect of caring for a totally dependent little human being! In those days of anxious waiting, when I was overdue at 41+ weeks, I couldn't face church, because everyone would be asking if I was still here (The bump in front meant that question didn't even need to be asked!) I listened to a tape from church on those verses we've read – Matthew 6:25-34 – Jesus' teaching on worry.

He said, "Do not worry about your life" (Matthew 6:25 –NIV) Worry never solves a problem – it just makes things worse. Worrying doesn't change a thing- it doesn't alter the length of our life by one second! Our times are in God's hands! If God looks after the birds of the air and the flowers in the field, how much more can He be trusted to look after us? Our God who created us in love can be trusted with the details of our life- He is intimately concerned about us, and He is powerful enough to meet our needs.

"O you of little faith" Jesus rebuked (Matthew 6:30-NIV) For worry boils down to little, limited faith, and little faith leads to a lot of worries as we fail to take God at His Word, and trust His promises. Jesus said, "Do not let your hearts be troubled and do not be afraid"

(John 14:27-NIV)

We don't have to fret about everyday life – about what we'll wear or what we'll eat, for 'Your heavenly Father already knows all your needs, and he will give you all you need from day to day if you live for him and make the Kingdom of God your primary concern'

(Matthew 6:32&33 – NLT)

We must turn our worries into prayers. Paul exhorts us- 'Don't worry about anything; instead, pray about everything' (Philippians 4:6 –NLT) If something is big enough to worry about, it's big enough to pray about! 'Let petitions and praises shape your worries into prayers, letting God know your concerns'

(Philippians 4: 6-The Message)

And when we 'tell God what you need and thank him for all he has done', (Philippians 4: 6 -NLT) we have got to leave the worries there with God. 'Cast all your anxiety on him because he cares for you' (I Peter 5:7-NIV), 'and he will sustain you'

(Psalm 55:22-NIV)

Another lesson I learnt when I was thrust into the throes of motherhood, was to take one day at a time-thinking beyond that just was overwhelming and too much to deal with! After all, today is the tomorrow we worried about yesterday! 'So don't be anxious about tomorrow. God will take care of your tomorrow too. Live one day at a time'   (Matthew 6:34 –TLB)

If we do this, we 'will experience God's peace, which is far more wonderful than the human mind can understand' (Philippians 4: 7-NLT) 'Before you know it, a sense of God's wholeness, everything coming together for good, will come and settle you down. It's wonderful what happens when Christ displaces worry at the centre of your life' (Philippians 4:7 –The Message) 'And the peace of God which transcends all understanding, will guard your hearts and your minds in Christ Jesus'

(Philippians 4:7 –NIV)

The peace of God-
- it calms the storms of life
- it soothes inner turmoil
- it quietens nagging doubts
- it stills restless spirits
- it nurses our souls into contented rest

'I don't concern myself with matters too great or awesome for me. But I have stilled and quietened myself, just as a small child is quiet with its mother' (Psalm 131:1&2 –NLT) 'I've cultivated a quiet heart. Like a baby content in its mother's arms, my soul is baby content'   (Psalm 131:2-The Message)

God, help me not to worry, but to simply just trust. Help me to take everything in my stride, hand in hand with You. May I gain confidence from You and trust You to provide – for You know all my needs, even before I ask.

Help me not to dwell on anxious thoughts that plague me – but rather to turn worries into prayers. Help me not to listen to Satan's lies- but to trust in Your truth –that I can do all things in You – with Your help and strength.

God, help me to really grasp and believe this. Help me to really enjoy life in You, the true life You died to give me- free from worry and doubt. My future is in Your hands, and You will take care of me tomorrow, just as You have today and yesterday.

Today, may I find my confidence in You. May I trade my anxieties and insecurities for your deep shalom peace.

'I prayed to the Lord, and he answered me, freeing me from all my fears. Those who look to him for help will be radiant with joy'   (Psalm 34:4 –NLT)

'But the Lord watches over those who fear him, those who rely on his unfailing love'   (Psalm 33:18 –NLT)

Focus on blessings rather than worries!

Loving God means trusting Him when life hurts

Feeling abandoned – but never alone!

Readings: II Corinthians 4:8&9, Isaiah 43:1-3

I have dreaded my 30th birthday for a long time! I remember how much I hated turning from 19 to 20 and I am sure changing from twenty something to the big 3-0 will be even worse! But no matter how bad my 30th birthday is this year, I am sure it will not be as bad as my 29th. For 16th June 2003 was my worst birthday, in fact it was the worst day of my life so far.

On that day, I was admitted to Knockbracken– a psychiatric hospital. I had been struggling with severe mental illness for 7 months. I was anxious, depressed and even suicidal. I felt so alone. My husband was at home with my two small children, trying to explain "Mummy's gone to hospital because she's lost her smile" A lot of my family were away in America at a wedding. I felt so low as I looked around the grey walls of the ward, wondering how I was ever going to get out of this place. For the first time in my life I felt abandoned by God. The words "My God, my God, why have you forsaken me?" echoed through my mixed up mind.

Yet even in this deeply dark time, God's still small voice reminded me that Jesus knew how I was feeling. For on the cross, the cry from Jesus' anguished heart was "Eloi, Eloi, lama sabachthani?" which means "My God, my God, why have you forsaken me?" (Matthew 27:46) On the cross, to a much greater extent than we will ever know, Jesus felt abandoned by His Father God as He took on the sins of the world. And at that time, in the middle of my deep depression, I could take comfort from the fact that Jesus understood, that He could sympathise with my weaknesses

(Hebrews 4:15)

The next day Pastor Baird came to see me and read Isaiah 43 and the Word of the Lord was deeply comforting – 'But now, this is what the Lord says- He who created you, O Jacob, He who formed you, O Israel: "Fear not, for I have redeemed you; I have summoned you by name; you are mine. When you pass through the waters, I will be with you; and when you pass through the rivers, they will not sweep over you. When you walk through the fire, you will not be burned; the flames will not set you ablaze. For I am the Lord, your God, the Holy One of Israel, your Saviour" (Isaiah 43:1-3-NIV) The Message phrases those words this way- "Don't be afraid, I've redeemed you. I've called your name. You're mine. When you're in over your head, I'll be there with you. When you're in rough waters, you will not go down. When you're between a rock and a hard place, it won't be a dead end – Because I am your God, your personal God"

(Isaiah 43:1-3-The Message)

No matter how hard life gets, no matter how down we feel, no matter how much we feel on our own, we are **never** alone. God is there with us – in the middle of our troubles, heartache and despair. 'The Lord is close to the broken hearted; He rescues those who are crushed in spirit' (Psalm 34:18 – NLT) Like the footprints poem reminds us, in our darkest hour, when there is just one set of footprints in the sand, we are not alone, God is carrying us.

Slowly and steadily over the days, weeks and months, I began to feel better – thanks to God and a very supportive family (and of course medication and my psychiatrist too!) Looking back, I can see God's hand at work. I can see how He brought us through and how He taught me to rely on Him.

There are some things that can only be learnt in the middle of difficulties. When our backs are to the wall, we tend to fall to our knees. Our heart cries out to God and He hears us. There are treasures of darkness – times of feeling God close against the odds – character building, spiritually defining times.

And these dark threads are necessary in the tapestry of life. God, the Master Craftsman is working on us, His work of art – and the dark areas give depth and character to the tapestry of life. It's hard to see all this at the time, but at the end, when His work is complete, we'll gasp in awe and realise truly that our God does work together all things for the good of those who love Him (Romans 8:28) It is in the valleys of life (not the mountain tops) that the real fruit grows. And God wants us to be vibrant, productive, fruitful Christians.

A diamond sparkles best against a black background. God the Master Craftsman knows that we, His precious stones reflect His glory best when times are tough.

Yes, we may feel abandoned, but we are never alone. 'We are pressed on every side by troubles, but we are not crushed and broken. We are perplexed, but we don't give up and quit. We are hunted down, but God never abandons us. We get knocked down, but we get up again and keep going'

(II Corinthians 4: 8&9 NLT)

As I said before, it's just as well we don't know what is around the corner of life – and it is. But God knows, and He is holding us, leading us on. And all around, and underneath are His everlasting arms

(Deuteronomy 33:27)

In the midst of all our trouble,
Heartache and despair,
We have a God who stands beside us,
A Friend Who's always there,
A Hope when things seem hopeless,
A Faith when things go wrong,
A Love that will never fail us,
That's never been more strong!

'But He knows the way that I take; when He has tested me, I will come forth as gold'

(Job 23:10 – NIV)

'Consider it a sheer gift, friends, when tests and challenges come at you from all sides. You know that under pressure, your faith-life is forced into the open and shows its true colours. So don't try to get out of anything prematurely. Let it do its work so you become mature and well-developed, not deficient in any way.'

(James 1: 2-4 – The Message)

A prayer from the heart

Lord, I need You.
I need You now more than ever before.
I need You to minister to me-to help me
rise above the problems and difficulties of life.
I need You to fill up my emptiness, because
I'm completely wiped out and spent.
I need Your grace at this time of need.
I need to sense Your love now more than ever.
I need to feel Your arms of love around me, to enable
me to feel safe and secure, despite the turmoil around.
I need to be touched by You- so that
I can reach out to others.
I need Your strength at my time of weakness.
I need Your joy now, when life hurts deeply.
I need You to know the cry of my heart, a cry
so deep, so silent that no-one else hears.
I need Your patience to take one day at a
time, step by step with You.
Lord, I know that You are all-
sufficient. You are my All in all.
I CAN depend on You- my Rock,
my Song, my Awesome Father God.

(This prayer was scribbled in a journal in September 2004, during another hospital admission. It was truly a prayer from the heart,)

The words of our Father

"I am your fortress in times of trouble,
My love is the anchor when things go wrong,
You are precious and in all situations,
I am working to make you strong!

I am your Rock when life seems uncertain,
My presence will guide when things are unclear.
You are loved and in all your problems
You can trust and have nothing to fear.

I am your Helper in times of testing,
My strength shows up best when you are weak,
You are my child and through all the tough times,
You can know my strength whenever you seek"

P.S. My 30th birthday has long been and gone! We had a great barbeque-complete with an adult sized bouncy castle. It was a bright, sunny day- and more importantly there was sunshine in my heart- a complete contrast to my 29th!

Loving God means trusting His timing is best

Seasons of the heart

Readings: Ecclesiastes 3:1-11, Psalm 27

'There is a time for everything, a season for every activity under heaven' (Ecclesiastes 3:1 – NLT)

There's a chill in the air and summer has fallen from the trees, as the leaves make a russet carpet under our feet. It's unmistakably autumn! Yet, as the year draws to a close these days will give way to the frosty mornings and crisp, star filled nights of winter. And soon, as the new year rolls on, from the darkness, from the hard, dead ground, new life of spring will burst! Snowdrops, yellow daffodils and purple crocuses will appear!

Life has its seasons too- happy, long days like summer; mellow, golden days of harvest and thanksgiving like autumn; days of hopeful anticipation like spring.

But perhaps now it is winter in your heart. Times are dark. Everything seems gloomy. Life itself feels dead. It is hard to even imagine the warm summer sun as happiness is but a distant memory. You might even feel alone, abandoned by God Himself.

Yet even this wintertime of the soul will not last forever.

The natural world does not stay static. Just as the blackberries mark summer turning to autumn, so the daffodils herald the end of winter and the beginning of spring. As sure as dawn follows even the darkest night, winter must give way to spring.

Even now, in the cold, difficult days, God is at work. The Creator God who turns around the seasons will breathe spring life into this winter of the heart. Winter cannot last forever. The difficulties will "come to pass, not come to stay", as my husband's grand-mother used to say.

In the winter, look forward to spring – the season of new life, vibrant colours, renewed hope, joy, fresh vi-sion, ideas and creativity. God will give 'beauty for ashes, joy instead of mourning, praise instead of de-spair' (Isaiah 61:3- NLT) 'Your lives will begin to glow in the darkness, your shadowed lives will be bathed in sunlight. I will always show you where to go. I'll give you a full life in the emptiest of places' (Isaiah 58:10 &11 – The Message) For, 'God has made everything beautiful in its own time.' (Ecclesiastes 3:11 – NLT) 'Where once there were thorns, cypress trees will grow. Where briars grew, myrtles will sprout up. This miracle will bring great honour to the Lord's Name; it will be an everlasting sign of His power and love'

(Isaiah 56:13 – NLT)

In this wintertime of the soul, you may feel like an acorn quietly dying in the depths of the earth. Remem-ber, in **His** time you 'will be called oaks of righteousness, a planting of the Lord for the display of his splendour'

(Isaiah 61:3- NIV)

'See! The winter is past;
the rains are over and gone.
Flowers appear on the earth;
The season of singing has come'

(Song of Songs 2:4-NIV)

So, 'Wait for the Lord; be strong and take heart and wait
for the Lord'   (Psalm 27:14 – NIV)

And though it has been winter in your soul for such a
long time, you will begin to feel that spring **is** in the air!

Loving God means wholeheartedly living for Him

Big-hearted for God!

Reading: Deuteronomy 6: 5, Numbers 14:5-25

In Numbers 14, God describes Caleb as having a 'different spirit' (Num 14:24 HCSB) as he followed Him *completely*. In Numbers 32:12, we are told that Joshua and Caleb were the only Israelite men who followed the Lord *wholeheartedly* throughout their lives. Joshua and Caleb were able to see past the giants and the city walls to God Himself who had the answers and the resources.

It is always encouraging to see young Christians starting out with real zeal and enthusiasm. But I think it is even more challenging to see older Christians, who have been living life as an adventure with God for decades, with the same zeal and devotion. It is great to start the race well. But it's even better to finish it well too!

When I think of older (though very much young at heart) Christians who have really challenged me, I always think of three people that I met over a decade ago, in Thailand. At that time, Edna- grace was an OMF missionary. She ran the guesthouse at Manorom Christian Hospital when I was doing my medical elective there.

She comes into my head anytime I think of hospitality! For, although I'd travelled thousands of miles from home, I truly felt at home at the guesthouse! I can still remember the crisp gingham sheets on the bed, which I lay on to recover from the long-haul flight! And, as well as looking after my practical needs, Edna-grace took time to get to know me and the other guests. Just last month I got a letter from her, telling me how now as a 'Senior' she is serving God in her home church in Vancouver.

Alan and Maelynn Ellard have been missionaries in Thailand for many years. At a time when others might have been thinking about retirement, they stepped out into a new ministry. On World AIDS Day, December 1990, God challenged them about the 300,000+ Thai people infected with HIV. God led them to motivate and encourage Thai churches to reach out with compassion to these people. In 1992, ACET Thailand (AIDS Care Education and Training) was born- helping those affected by HIV and AIDS, showing God's love in action. At present, among many other things, they're building a new home for the House of Grace orphanage in Chantaburi, Thailand (Read the last page for more information!)

I guess living wholeheartedly for God means doing what He wants. 'Do not merely listen to the word, and so deceive yourselves. Do what it says' (James 1:22-NIV) It means obedience.

When I was at Dundee University, Joanne Ellis (an OMF missionary) spoke at the Christian Union. She said, "It's not brilliance God wants – just simple obedience. Listen to that still small voice and once you hear it, let nothing move you, the glory of God is at stake. We need holy determination to see God's purposes for the nations fulfilled in our generation. It's a matter of simple, quick obedience"

Sometimes we make things more complicated than God intended them to be! Obedience really just means finding out what God thinks and doing what He says.

A few months ago, the kids brought up the topic of 'bad words'! They were discussing if 'O my word' was all right to say- as one of their friends had said it wasn't. Ethan (aged 4) disappeared into his room for a couple of minutes. He re-emerged with a smile on his face. "It's O.K.! O my word is O.K. I've just asked God, and He said it's O.K.!"

The debate was over - as Ethan had done what we as adults so often forget to do. He had consulted God for His view and acted on it. 'It is enough to simply ask the Father' as Amy Carmichael said.

Loving God does mean obedience. 'Those who say they live in God should live their lives as Christ did.'

(I John 2:6-NLT)

'Those who catch the vision are ready to follow the Lamb, wherever He goes, regardless of what following may involve for them. They are given the power to fulfil their high calling. They are those who have the courage to break conventialities, who care not at all what the world thinks of them, because they are entirely taken up with the realities of the soul and God'

(Bishop Bardsley)

'Teach me your way, O Lord,
and I will walk in your truth;
give me an undivided heart,
that I may fear your name.'

(Psalm 86:11-NIV)

'Not everyone will do big things but everyone can do small things with a big heart'   (Bob Gass)[3]

'May you hear His voice and return His love with your life'   (Angela Thomas)[4]

A prayer of commitment

O God – my God and my Father,
I praise You for all You have freely given
to me, and I freely give it all back to You.
All that I have.
All that I am.
All of my dreams and aspirations.
All of my fears and anxieties.
All my weaknesses and failings.
All the bad times and all the good times.
All those who are close to my heart
– my husband, my children and my family.

I commit them all to Your loving watch-care, today and every day.

I commit each day to You, Lord, that I'd truly live for You - that I'd be a woman after Your own heart, that my heart would beat in time with Yours; that my life's music would be in harmony with worship to You; that I'd reflect Your glory and shine Your love- just where I am, because that's where You want me to be.

So, I give myself to You as a tool You can use to build Your kingdom, as an instrument to play Your love-song to the world.

With Your help, I can do **all** things. You are my **All-in-All.**

'And God is able to make **all** grace abound to you, so that in **all** things at **all** times, having **all** that you need, you will abound in every good work' (II Corinthians 9:8)

The unashamed disciple

'I am a disciple of Jesus Christ. I won't look back, let up, slow down, back away, or be still. My past is redeemed, my present makes sense and my future is secure. I am finished and done with low living, sight walking, small planning, colourless dreams and dwarfed goals.

I no longer need position, promotion or popularity. I now live by presence, lean by faith, love by patience, lift by prayer, labour by power. My goal is heaven, my road is narrow, my way is rough, my companions few, my God reliable, my mission clear.

I cannot be bought, compromised, deterred, lured away, turned back, diluted or delayed. I will not flinch in the face of sacrifice, hesitate in the presence of adversity, ponder at the pool of popularity, or meander in the maze of mediocrity.

I am a disciple of Jesus Christ. I must go until heaven returns, give until I drop, preach until all know and work until he comes. And when He comes to get His own, He will have no problem recognising me. My colours will be clear' (Author Unknown)

'We love because he first loved us'   (I John 4:19-NIV)

PART 3

LOVING GOD
MEANS LOVING OTHERS

"A new commandment I give you: Love one another.
As I have loved you, so you must love one another.
By this all men will know that you are
my disciples, if you love one another"
(John 13:34&35 –NIV)

'Dear friends, since God so loved us,
we ought also to love one another. No one
has ever seen God; but if we love one another,
God lives in us and his love is made complete in us'
(I John 4:12-NIV)

Loving God means loving our husbands

A three stranded cord

Reading: Ephesians 5:22-33

Loving God means loving others. The love that God has poured into our loves must overflow into the lives of others. And first and foremost, we must love those close to us. Paul says in Titus 2:4 that the younger women should love their husbands, and love their children – in that order.

During Easter 2004 we had a family break to Scotland. We went to Loch Katrine in the Trossachs (probably the most beautiful Loch in the world- according to Rob!!) We hired a tandem with a trailer for the kids to sit in. I thought it was a good illustration of family life!

The husband and wife have to be co-operating and both doing their part- cycling in tandem for the family to go in the right direction. The husband may be the one at the front, leading the way. But the wife has to make the effort, to help her husband and play her part by pedalling. When this happens, the children will relax and just enjoy the ride!

But if mum and dad are arguing and disagreeing, pedalling in opposite directions, the family unit won't move anywhere fast!

Someone has wisely said, "The best thing you can do for your children is to love their dad"

In Greek, there are four words for love – phileo (friendship love), storge (family love), eros (sexual love) and agape (unconditional love) We should love our husbands in all four ways – after all, he should be our best friend, the most important member of our family, our lover, and our gift from God Himself.

Some days we find loving our husbands easier than others. There are so many guy-girl differences! After all- men are from Mars and women are from Venus- al-legedly! They just don't get chick flicks, the need for pretty wrapping on presents and the dark/lights/whites concept for sorting washing! Bickering sometimes seems easier than communicating!

However, 'love pulls a quilt over the bickering'
(Proverbs 10:12-The Message)

Loving our husband means:
- making him feel appreciated
- putting his needs before our own
- respecting him and not putting him
  down in front of others
- not arguing in front of the kids
- cooking his favourite meal
- giving him space to grow
- communicating how we feel
- meaning what we say, saying what we mean
- allowing him a lie-in
- continuing to have special 'dates'
- going to bed at the same time
- leaving dirty boots at the door i.e. when we've had a

bad day, we need to leave the bad mood at the door instead of walking all around the house in it!

- avoid criticising, for criticism 'strips the trees of both the blossoms and the caterpillars together!'
- having God at the centre of the relationship - after all marriage was His idea!

And I don't think that it's too simplistic to say that God's idea of marriage is a matter of 1-2-3:

1. 'Two become **one**' (Matthew 19:6- NIV) Marriage means unity-not living separate lives together under the same roof. Not just existing and surviving side by side- but thriving, growing and developing. Not being distant - but really connecting- emotionally, spiritually and physically- living in true unity.

2. '**Two** are better than one' (Ecclesiastes 4:9-NIV) 'Two people can accomplish more than twice as much as one' (Ecclesiastes 4:9-NLT) i.e. synergy- we achieve more together than merely the sum of what we have could have done alone.

3. But three are even better: 'A cord of **three** strands is not quickly broken' (Ecclesiastes 4:12- NIV) That's God in the equation! With our Almighty God at the centre of our marriage, we have strength and endurance for times of testing. We can accomplish what seems impossible to outsiders! It's a three-part harmony. It's a triangular relationship –the closer we grow to God, the closer we grow to each other. It's marriage as God intended it to be!

The reading today, Ephesians 5, may seem a little old-fashioned- totally different to 21st century ideas. Yet, it's

God's blueprint for relationships in the home- to bring harmony and stability and to create the right environment for raising children. This passage was read at our friends, Jo and Andy's wedding, from The Message translation. Try to read it again in this thought-provoking version.

In the passage, we are given insight as to what it means to submit to our husbands- 'Wives understand and support your husbands in ways that show your support for Christ' (Ephesians 5:22-The Message) If that seems like a tall order, read what our husbands are called to do- 'Husbands go all out in your love for your wives, exactly as Christ did for the church- a love marked by giving, not getting.' (Ephesians 5:25-The Message) Wow!

Stormie Omartian[1] says, 'Part of making a house a home is allowing your husband to be the head, so that you can be the heart'[1] I think that she gives good insight into how things were designed to be!

God wants us to share life together as a great adventure!

And, 'Do two walk together unless they have agreed to do so?' (Amos 3:3-NIV)

So, if you feel that you are walking in opposite directions, as Mr and Mrs, remember, 'A journey of a thousand miles begins with one step!' (Chinese Proverb) And think, what small step can you take today to start the adventure together, or to make a good marriage better?

Loving our husbands means praying for them

A prayer for my husband

O Father God,

I pray for my husband today. May he know how precious he is – he's Your precious son – bought at a price, loved with everlasting love, made for Your pleasure. He is precious to us – as head of our family. He is the rock that brings stability, the figure that brings security. He's the one the children run to when he comes in the door. He's the one I run to for help and encouragement.

May he feel blessed by You. May he sense his incredible worth in Your eyes. May he realise his purpose in You. May he grasp the destiny he has in You. Give him vision, ambition and fulfilment. May he do his best, and put his whole heart into his job – working for you, not men and women. May he make an impact on people he meets, pointing them to You. May he be a real man of God, who truly seeks Your face, searches for your heart and follows Your direction.

May he feel your Father-love, that he in turn would be a daddy that our kids can respect and admire – a dad that reveals His Heavenly Father to their young hearts.

May he have a close circle of family and friends with strong bonds of true love. Yet, may he realise that You alone are the Friend that sticks closer than a brother.

May I be the wife that he needs. Help me to be his best friend, and true help-mate. Help me to listen, encourage, build up and spur on. Help us to work together as a partnership – that our home would be a happy one where we can nurture our children. May we join our hands together, for two are better than one. And may we join our hands to Yours, for a three stranded cord is not easily broken.

May he know today and every day that he is loved – by You and us. May he feel 'prayed for' and joyful today.

In Jesus' Name,

Amen

Loving God means loving our children

Love that gives, and keeps on giving

Readings: Titus 2:4&5, Psalm 127 & 128

Love for our children begins even before they're born. With each flutter of movement, each tiny kick and hiccough that we feel while they're inside, deep love wells up. And often we're overwhelmed with incredible love the moment they're born, in those first moments that we gaze at our precious newborn child, and hold our delicate little bundle of joy!

And they're precious in God's eyes too. 'Children are a gift from God, they are a reward from him' (Psalm 127:3 – NLT) What an awesome privilege and responsibility we have as parents. God Himself has entrusted our little ones into our care.

Some days it's easy to love them! They do what we ask and they're easy to please. The sun is shining, the birds are singing and life is beautiful! Other days are different-breakfast is splattered across the floor, toothbrushes end up down the toilet and the entire toilet roll is unravelled through all the upstairs rooms. Often it's a day of the terrible Ts – temper tantrums, teething or toilet training! (That book 'Potty training in a week' should be banned!)

As a T-shirt slogan read, they go from 'nought to naughty in 30 seconds!' and as someone said 'Where there's a will, there's a won't!' Our patience is tested, our nerves are shattered and we are just about ready to explode! Even at times like this, our call is to love our children.

Our love should be practical – changing nappies, wiping noses, bathing, clothing and feeding.

Our love should be watchful – looking after them and looking out for them.

Our love should be tough – we must love them enough to discipline them, to make them better little people.

Our love should be prayerful – surrounding their daily lives with our Father's watch care.

Our love should be playful- getting down to their level, and learning to laugh with them.

But above all, our love should be unconditional – a love like God's. Many love conditionally- "I love you because" or "I love you if" or "I love you when". With our children, it's got to be "I love you". Period. Love with no strings or expectations attached. Love, no matter what. Love that gives, and keeps on giving.

Psalm 128:7 in the Message describes our children as being 'as fresh and promising as young olive shoots' Our little ones have such God given potential - if nurtured in the right environment. 'When the water of love is given, your child will bloom and bless the world with beauty'

(The Five Love Languages of Children)[2]

'Children grow with milk and praise!'

'So don't get tired of doing what is good. Don't get discouraged and give up, for we will reap a harvest of blessing at the appropriate time' (Galatians 6:9-NLT) 'So don't get tired of making up bottles, changing nappies, picking up toys, cooking, cleaning and reading that story over and over again. You will enjoy God's blessing in days ahead, if you keep on loving!'

(Galatians 6:9-Coulter paraphrase 2007!)

'Duty makes us do things well, but love makes us do them beautifully' (Philip Brooks)

'A mum is God's love in action.
She looks with her heart,
And feels with her eyes.
A mum is the bank where her children
deposit all their worries and hurt.
A mum is the cement that keeps her family together,
And her love lasts a lifetime.'

(Sent as a text from Julie Allen-Oct 2006)

'A mother's love is the heart of the home'

Loving our children means sasking God for help

There's no place like home!

Reading: Proverbs 31:10-31

Society tells us that we can have it all – a successful career, a wonderful family, a picture perfect home and a beautiful body! You can be a domestic goddess, a supermum and a wonder woman! You can have a perfect home where the ironing gets done, wholesome home cooked meals are served, the children are always clean, wearing clothes that match and the rooms are always tidy! Breakfast time looks like an ad from a cereal box and each day runs like clockwork! Sorry to shatter any illusions but real life isn't like this – if yours is, let me know!

I didn't learn how to juggle until I became a mum! Now it's hard to imagine life B. C. (Before Children) and I wonder what I used to do with my time! Life is so busy, busy, busy! Going out the front door is a major expedition. Preparing dinner with a bambino in your arms and a toddler round your feet is an accomplishment. In fact some days, just being able to grab breakfast and a shower feels like a major achievement! Doing ten things simultaneously is what we mothers do best!

But multitasking is not a modern phenomenon! Just reading about the wife of noble character in Proverbs

31 makes me feel tired! This woman got up before dawn and worked late into the night. She was a hard worker whose hands were always busy – spinning wool, making garments, preparing breakfast, buying fields, providing warm clothes for her family and reaching out to the needy. She was an energetic, industrious woman who really knew how to get things done! She was worth far more than precious rubies!

(Proverbs 31:10)

But our focus must not just be task orientated. If it is, we'll just end up frustrated, for as the saying goes: 'A woman's work is never done!' No matter how clean and tidy our house is one day, it'll have the lived-in look again the next! There'll always be more washing-up to do, more bottles to make up, more nappies to change, more meals to cook.

Someone once said that there is no way to be a perfect mum but a million ways to be a good one! I would go further and say that even more important than being a good mum is being a godly one. The conclusion of the book of Proverbs states, 'Charm is deceptive and beauty is fleeting; but a woman who fears the Lord is to be praised'   (Proverbs 31:30-NIV)

The task of raising children is an awesome one. We simply cannot do it on our own – we need God-sized help. We must be in daily contact with our Heavenly Father who is the only Perfect Parent. We need His wisdom as we encounter every day situations and He has promised to give it to us, if we only ask (James 1:5) We need 'love, joy, peace, patience, kindness, goodness, faithfulness, gentleness and self- control' (Galatians 5:22 &23 -NIV) – the fruit of Spirit – which grows from being connected to God the Vine.

If we seek to be godly mums, our houses may not always be spotless, we may not ever get to the bottom of the ironing basket, our bathrooms may not shimmer and shine. But, our priorities will be right. We will become homemakers rather than stress generators. Our children will know the blessing of having a mum who is a woman after God's heart and we will be able to point their hearts toward Him too.

If we seek to be godly mums, the rest will follow, for a happy home has God at the centre.

'If you look after what is dear to God, He will look after what is dear to you!'

The twenty first century supermum

What makes a great wife and mum?
She's hard to find these days!
Her husband trusts her completely,
and she enriches his life,
supporting him and never undermining him.

Costumes for the school play? She's happy to help-
knows just where to get the stuff they need ,
and stays up very late (again!) making them.

She's organised about her food shopping,
recycles as much as possible, does a part-time job,
and grows what she can in the garden.

This woman makes sure she stays fit and healthy,
keeps an eye on where the money goes-
and never forgets to take the bread out of the freezer!

She always has some project in hand,
is generous and enthusiastic to a fault
and concerned for Fair Trade and the world's poor.

She doesn't worry when winter arrives because
she gently reminded her husband (twice) a few months ago
to check that the central heating was working.
She puts her practical gifts to good use
in making a comfortable home
and contributing to the family income.

She dresses well, without ostentation,
and her husband is held in respect
in the church and the community.

She has presence and inner strength,
facing the future whatever it may hold,
with calm-and a sense of humour.

She never gives advice unasked,
but is known for her wisdom and common sense
and can be relied on for an honest opinion.

She is always busy, never idle,
keeping track of everyone and everything
so that family life runs smoothly.

She can find geometry sets and football boots,
remembers to record that important TV programme,
and writes regularly to her children at university.

Her family finally appreciate her,
recognising all she has done for them;
they tell her she's great- and mean it!

Her husband actually puts it into words too-
'Lots of women have busy, useful lives,
but you are the best and I love you'

Charm is superficial, and beauty skin-deep,
but the woman who honours God in her family life
will have something more lasting- an eternal reward'
(Christine Orme)[3]

'It's not what you do but how much love you put into it
that counts' (Mother Theresa)

Loving our children
means showing them Jesus

Teachable moments!

Readings: Deuteronomy 6: 4-9, II Timothy 1:3-7

As Christian parents, our awesome responsibility is to pass on our faith to our children. 'Let every generation tell its children of your mighty acts' (Psalm 145:4 – NLT) In our homes we have the God-given opportunity to live out our faith, to give our children a spiritual heritage. Going to church is important, but home is where they see God's love in action   (or not) – 24-7.

> Whatever we do, they're watching us:
> *'How careful then I ought to be;*
> *A little one now follows me.*
> *I do not dare to go astray,*
> *For fear she'll go the self-same way.*
> *I cannot once escape her eyes,*
> *For what she sees me do she tries.*
> *She thinks that I am good and fine,*
> *Believes in every word of mine.*
> *I must remember as I go,*
> *Through summer's sun or winter's snow,*
> *I'm building for the years to be,*
> *The little one who follows me'*
>
> *(Author Unknown)*

Yes, our children don't miss a thing. They pick up on our habits – both good and bad. Our actions must back up our words and our behaviour must match up with our beliefs. How we talk on the phone is therefore as important as how we talk to God.

On holiday, in Cork last summer, I was at the park with our kids one evening. There was another mum there. We got chatting, and I knew she was a Christian, before she said she was, by the patient, gentle way she was talking to her children. I felt quite challenged!

We must tell our children that we love them. We must tell them that God loves them. But more importantly, we've got to show it – to reveal the amazing love of God to their eyes. Our children can see His love in our eyes and can sense His love in our actions.

God's love cannot be confined to church on Sunday. It must be translated into everyday life. As Moses wrote in Deuteronomy, we've got to impress God's instruction on our children, and talk about it when we're at home, when we're out and about, when we lie down and when we get up. In other words, wherever we are, we bring God with us. In every situation, He can be involved. In our daily activity, there can be teachable moments.

We can point out creation and introduce the Creator to our children- as we walk along Ballywalter Beach, or around the lake at Mount Stewart. We can pray in the car. We can pray for our children and more importantly, we can pray with them. By doing so, prayer will become an integral part of their life too. I smothered a smile as I overheard our not-quite-three-year-old praying that God would help her not to be cheeky!

If our children see that our faith is a real, life-affecting entity, they will embrace it too, and take it on board at their own level. Caris' first prayer was "God help mummy, baby!" when she wasn't even 2 and I was going to hospital to have Ethan. One day, when she was a toddler Caris exclaimed, "I love Jesus, and I want to give Him a big hug!" When we lost our peeler around that time, she said, "Maybe Jesus took it to peel apples for all His children!" And Ethan used to make us smile when he first started saying grace by praying, "Thank you God for doggie food and real food!"

I believe that God wants our faith to be more like theirs-honest, simple and trusting.

II Timothy 1:5 & 3:15 tell us how Timothy's mother and grandmother passed their faith onto him. He was taught the Bible as a child and by trusting Jesus, he made their faith his own. We too need to break God's Word into child-sized chunks! Like little sponges they will absorb its truth in their formative years. And I believe they will give their lives over to Jesus at their God-appointed time!

Lord,

I thank you for our children, these little ones that you have entrusted into our care- a precious gift from you.

Thank You Father that You are there watching over our children when we are not. Protect them Lord from harm and danger.

Parenting is a daunting task yet, I thank you that you are a Perfect Father-our Abba, Daddy. We can ask you for wisdom and you have promised to guide and direct.

May we be more like You- slow to anger, quick to listen and abounding in love.

Give us self-control and gentleness, even when our patience is being stretched by demands and demanding little ones. Help me to pause, rather than explode.

May they see Your love, joy, peace and patience in us. May I introduce them to You.

May they come to You when they are still young and live their whole lives for you, growing big and strong in You. Keep their hearts turned towards you all of their days, that they too may live a life of love.

Amen

'Blessed are the mothers of the earth, for they have combined the practical and the spiritual into one work-able way of human life. They have darned little stock-ings, mended little dresses, washed little faces, and have pointed little eyes to the stars and little souls to eternal things.'   (William L. Stidger)

Loving our family
means praying for them

A mother's prayer

Dear Father,

I want to me a woman of God- whose heart is fully devoted to You, whose life is lived totally for you, whose home shines for you, whose family impacts the world for you, whose love reaches out across the street and across the globe for you.

I want my husband to know the blessing of having a spirit filled wife- for home to be a place of refreshment.

I want our children to have a mum who is Christ- like in her attitudes. I want them to see Your love, joy and patience demonstrated in me. I want to point them to You everyday, from now on, so that while they are still young they will come to know you for themselves.

I want to cast all my cares and anxieties on you- if something is big enough to worry about, it's big enough to pray about!

Help me God. I can't do it on my own. I need You now, more than ever. I need You everyday-

I need Your joy to brighten each day.
I need Your strength to fulfil Your plan for me each day.

I need Your love to pass on unconditionally
to my children each day.
I need Your grace to relate to others each day.
I need Your wisdom to deal with decisions each day.
I need Your patience when mine is stretched each day.
I need Your peace to take away worries each day.
I need Your hope each day – for my future
is as bright as the promises of God!
I need Your power to make me strong.
I need Your joy to make life a song.
I need Your forgiveness when it all goes wrong.
I need You Lord, everyday, my whole life long!

Thank You God that You are so near – just a prayer away. Help me to hear Your heart beat, that my life would echo it. May I act like your daughter. May I be the mother you want me to be. May I live a life of love-following in Your footprints, leaving Your fragrance, showing Your grace and shining Your light.

In Jesus' precious Name,

Amen

Loving God means showing love in our home

Home sweet home

Reading: I Corinthians 13

'A wise woman builds her house' (Proverbs 14:1- NLT) A wise woman builds her home, not with bricks and mortar, but with love- love like God's. The atmosphere should be saturated with love like His.

Home-

It's the place where you can be yourself, where you can kick your shoes off, put your feet up and relax and unwind.

It's an oasis in dry times.

It's the greenhouse where the fruit of the spirit is cultivated.

It's the shed where broken hearts and broken dreams are mended.

It's the retreat where life's hurts are soothed away

It's a safe haven from life's storms.

It's the place we all need to come back to, out of the stress, so that we can go out and face it all again the next day.

It's the nursery where little lives are nurtured, and big questions are answered.

It's the sanctuary where prayer is humbly offered, where praise to God resounds.

It's the first place of ministry, where we show our servant heart.

It's the open door where outsiders are welcomed in, to spend time and go out again refreshed.

It's a little piece of heaven on earth, for God is in the midst of it. Indeed He must be the foundation for, 'Unless the Lord builds the house its builders labour in vain'
(Psalm 127:1 –NIV)

Home should be the perfect environment for little ones to thrive- for little minds to flourish. Home should foster individuality and encourage creativity to flow. It should be a forum of open communication and mutual encouragement. There, each family member should realise their worth in God's and each other's eyes.

The wise woman builds up a home where love lives. In the house where love lives, there's no place for raised voices or stamping feet. There's no room for bickering and yelling. The sound of the door slamming isn't heard in the house where love lives. Nor is the cold, stony silence of sulking. Getting out of the wrong side of bed, having P.M.T. or having a short fuse and a quick temper is no excuse. We've got to work on it. We must 'be quick to listen, slow to speak and slow to become angry' (James 1:17-NIV) 'Do not let the sun go down while you are still angry' (Ephesians 4:26 – NIV) We can't stop the sun from going down, but we can patch up differences and go to sleep with a clear conscience. After all, ' Love covers all wrongs' (Proverbs 10:12 -NIV)- like a cosy quilt!

In the home where love lives, there is no place for sarcasm or criticism. How quickly a happy atmosphere disintegrates with harsh words. It evaporates with unkind comments. How easily the mood of the whole family can be lowered if we as wives and mothers are in a bad mood. As someone once said- "If momma ain't happy, nobody's happy!" Love leads to peace, and 'A meal of bread and water in contented peace is better than a banquet spiced with quarrels.' (Proverbs 17:1 –The Message)

In the home where love lives, there is no nagging! (It doesn't work, anyway!) For, 'Better to live alone in a tumbledown shack than share a mansion with a nagging spouse' (Proverbs 21:9 –The Message) Elsewhere in Proverbs (19:13), it says that a nagging wife is like a dripping tap. We've had a dripping tap in our kitchen, and I know just how annoying that sound is!

In the home where love lives, the rooms are brightened with smiles. The walls resound with praise. Laughter is heard. Joy is evident, for ' A glad heart makes a happy face' (Proverbs 15:13-NLT). The words "I love you" are often heard. So is "Sorry" – for we all inevitably mess up sometimes. Words of affirmation and appreciation build up the home where love lives. Prayers are offered, for if God is the foundation, prayer is the cement that keeps the family together. In the home where love lives, the ambience comes from God Himself.

Yes, the wise woman builds a home where love lives for, 'Love is patient, love is kind. It does not envy, it does not boast, it is not proud. It is not rude, it is not self-seeking, it is not easily angered, it keeps no record of wrongs. Love does not delight in evil, but rejoices with the truth. It always protects, always trusts, always hopes, always perseveres. Love never fails'

(I Corinthians 13:4-8 –NIV)

O God, I commit our home to you. May You be the foundation. May it be built in love and cemented in prayer. May it be a home where love lives. In it, may we encourage each other and nurture our children. From it, may we reach out to others.

'Love in the home=joy in the heart!'

P.S. I've just re-read this section entitled 'Home Sweet Home', and all I can say is 'Wow!' I fall so far short of my own ideals, never mind God's! All too often, my house is not where love lives. Love (temporarily) leaves the building, fleeing from my explosive temper and angry outbursts. As I read the above words that I wrote a couple of years ago, I'm praying to God to help me make my home a place where love lives, more often than not!

Love- a variation on a theme

If I live in a house of spotless beauty with everything in its place, but have not love, I am a housekeeper- not a home-maker.

If I have time for waxing, polishing, and decorative achievements, but have not love, my children learn of cleanliness – not godliness.

> Love leaves the dust in search of a child's laugh.
> Love smiles at the tiny fingerprints
> on a newly cleaned window.
> Love wipes away the tears before it wipes
> up the spilled milk.
> Love picks up the child before it picks up the toys.
> Love is present through the trials.

Love reprimands, reproves and is responsive.
Love crawls with the baby, walks with the
toddler, runs with the child, then stands
aside to let the youth walk into adulthood.
Love is the key that opens salvation's
message to a child's heart.

Before I became a mother I took glory in my house of
perfection. Now I glory in God's perfection of my child.

As a mother there is much I must teach my child, but
the greatest of all is love.'

(Jo Ann Merrell)[4]

Loving others means being a blessing

Blessed 2 B a blessing!

Readings: Genesis 12:1-3, Matthew 5:13-16

The call of Abram in Genesis 12 is often used to empha-sise going to serve God overseas. After all, God said in verse 1 – "Leave your country, your people and your father's house and go to the land I will show you." But perhaps the most important thing is not where we go but what we are. For God continues, "I will bless you and you will be a blessing" (v2). The bottom line is – are we prepared to allow God to use us to bless others just where we are? The geography of whereabouts we are on this planet doesn't matter, but the attitude of our heart does.

We have been given so much – every spiritual bless-ing in Christ and so many material things too. We have been given much and in turn we should give much to others. God holds us responsible to use our gifts, talents and resources effectively. Jesus said, "From everyone who has been given much, much will be demanded; and from the one who has been entrusted with much, much more will be asked."   (Luke 12: 48b – NIV)

We can either be a vase or a bucket. A vase may be pretty to look at, but doesn't actually do much, while a bucket is not usually admired, but is very useful, bringing water where it is needed. God wants us to be buckets – bringing the Water of Life to those we meet. For, 'He who refreshes others will himself be refreshed'

(Proverbs 11:25- NIV)

We cannot keep God's blessing to ourselves or we will become stagnant. God wants us to be vibrant, contagious Christians – life-enhancers, brightening the corner just where we are, shining like stars in the universe against the back drop of darkness (Philippians 2:15) God wants us 'to be light, bringing out the God-colours in the world' and 'to be salt-seasoning that brings out the God-flavours in this earth' (Matthew 5:13&14-The Message)

God has lavished His extravagant, amazing, everlasting love and grace on us and we cannot keep it to ourselves. It must overflow to those around us – in our home first and foremost – then to all our circle of influence. Then our husbands will feel valued, our children will feel accepted, our friends will feel refreshed and all will see Jesus in us!

'Keep open house; be generous with your lives. By opening up to others, you'll prompt people to open up with God, this generous Father in heaven'

(Matthew 5:16-The Message)

Lord, we have been blessed with much, and we give ourselves and our things back to You, to use. It's all Yours anyway!

'Love isn't love till you give it away!' (Mother Theresa)

We should be so excited by the grace of God that we cannot keep it to ourselves!

'Bloom where you are planted!'

Loving others means praying for them

Prayer is like a telephone!

Readings: Ephesians 1:15-23,Colossians 1:1-14

'Prayer is like a telephone so we can talk to God!' the kids' chorus says. It's like a mobile phone we can use at any time, a direct line to our Father in heaven. Yet, how many of us pray even half as much as we text or talk on our mobile phone?

There are many books out there on prayer, and they would teach much more about prayer than I can in the next few lines. Many of us, especially me, find our prayer lives a struggle and we spend so much less time in prayer than we mean too. Often, I find myself praying, like the disciples "Lord, teach us to pray!"

When we were younger, many of us prayed "God bless everyone in the whole wide world! Amen!" That just about covers everyone, but it's not really very specific!

Recently, Paul's prayers in his letters in the New Testament have challenged me. Maybe we should pray for others as he did. If we pray specifically, as Paul did, God would bless our friends and family.

We should start by thanking God for them (Ephesians 1:16) 'I thank my God every time I remember you'

(Philippians 1:3-NIV) He thought of their faithful work, their loving deeds and their hope (I Thessalonians 1:3) He was thankful that their faith was flourishing and their love for each other was increasing (II Thessalonians 1:3) We too can thank God for the good characteristics in our friends and family.

He remembered them in prayer (Ephesians 1:16) In Romans 1: 9, he said that God was his witness to how constantly he remembered them in his prayers, at all times. How often do we pray for others, those close to our hearts, those working across the globe for our God, those brothers and sisters suffering because of their beliefs?

What specifically did Paul pray for? How can we pray for those God has brought into our lives? We can pray that:

- they would know God better   (Ephesians 1:17)
- the eyes of their heart would be opened (Ephesians 1:18) so they can see clearly what God wants them to do.
- they will have hope and be sure of their inheritance (Ephesians 1:18) 'I pray that your hearts will be flooded with light so that you can understand the wonderful future he has promised to those he called. I want you to realize what a rich and glorious inheritance he has given to his people'

  (Ephesians 1:18 NLT)
- they would realise the immensity of God's power available to them (Ephesians 1:19) and be strengthened by it (Colossians1:11) their love would abound more and more in knowledge and depth of insight, that they would be discerning, pure and fruitful (Philippians 1:9) 'So this is my prayer: that

your love will flourish and that you will not only love much but well'
(Philippians 1:9-The Message)

- they will know God's will and live to please Him
(Colossians 1:10)
- they will bear fruit and grow (Colossians 1:10) and be vibrant Christians.
- they will be patient (Colossians 1:11)
- they will be thankful to God (Colossians 1:12)
- they will be active in sharing their faith
(Philemon 1:6)

There is no limit to what we can pray for. Pray 'as deep as your heart and as wide as your world'
(Fern Nichols)[5]

Paul urges 'Pray hard and long' (Ephesians 6:18-The Message) We must P.U.S.H - Pray Until Something Happens!

'In prayer there is a connection between what God does and what you do' (Matthew 6:14-The Message) We have no idea how our prayers will impact others, as the following story illustrates:

'It was night time in mid-September. Miss Piu, a young Laotian believer, stood on the banks of the surging Mekong River.

She had just called her family from a pay phone to say goodbye. And now she was ready to throw herself into the river to end her life.

Beside themselves with worry, her family called their Christian friends and asked them to pray.

And 12 time zones away in America, God himself called an intercessor to her knees and prompted her to pray too.

As believers prayed around the globe, the clouds in the dark sky above the Mekong River parted. Looking up, Miss Piu saw a single bright star.

She turned around and headed away from the river. Away from death and towards a new life with God.

With the God who had sent a single bright star as a sign of his love for her'

(East Asia's Billions)[6]

'I urge you, brothers, by our Lord Jesus Christ and by the love of the Spirit, to join me in my struggle by praying to God for me.' (Romans 15:30-NIV)

Loving others means showing them Jesus

Fragrant aromas

Reading: II Corinthians 2:14&15

It's amazing how scents can awaken our senses and evoke powerful memories! Cinnamon and pine reminds us of Christmas. There's no smell as sweet or innocent as the baby fresh smell of baby bath oil. I love the welcoming aroma of home-baked bread and freshly ground coffee. Lavender is great for a calming and relaxed atmosphere. It's comforting to smell our husband's aftershave lingering on his shirts. And we all have a favourite perfume – or we may have several, and which one we choose depends on our mood!

The Bible says that 'we are to God the aroma of Christ' (II Corinthians 2:15 – NIV), for God 'through us spreads everywhere the fragrance of the knowledge of him' (II Corinthians 2:14-NIV) 'Everywhere we go, people breathe in the exquisite fragrance. Because of Christ, we give off a sweet scent rising to God'

(II Corinthians 2:15-The Message)

As we live our daily lives, we rub shoulders with people who don't know our God. If we love them with a love like God has for us, we will want to awaken their spiritual senses, we will want to evoke memories of things they've heard before. We will want the fragrant aroma of our Jesus to linger after we've moved on. We will want the scent of Christ to overpower the stench of sin, which is so evident all around.

After all, we are the only Bible some people will ever read – we are the message! Our lives can be a powerful testimony. St. Francis of Assisi said, "Preach the Gospel always, and when necessary use words!" We are the only Jesus some people will ever see. Indeed, the word Christian literally means 'mini-Christ'

Our lives must speak out - not for ourselves, but that others may see our good deeds and praise our Father in Heaven   (Matthew 5:16)

'Now wherever we go he uses us to tell others about the Lord and to spread the Good News like a sweet perfume. Our lives are a fragrance presented by Christ to God'   (II Corinthians 2:14&15-NLT)

Loving others means treating them like God wants us to

One anothers

Readings: John 17 & Philippians 2:1-11

Church. Not the bricks and mortar building, or the Sunday morning service - but the people. The living stones. The body of Christ. The called out and chosen ones ('Ekklesia' in Greek) The family of God.

As in every family, there are different personalities. The optimists and the pessimists. The introverts and the extroverts. The movers and shakers and the don't rock the boaters! The contemporary and the traditional. The saints and the sinners. The young at heart and the old before their time. The organ lovers and the drummers. The happy clappys and those whose face would surely crack if they attempted to smile in church!

And that's before we even get into doctrinal differences-but we won't even go there today!!

We talk about dysfunctional families - but how dysfunctional the family of God is at times. We as parents hate when our children bicker, squabble and argue. How far short we fall of God's view of the church as His body- connected to Jesus, the Head and working together in harmony- attaining so much more together than we ever could achieve working alone. It must grieve the Father-heart of our God when He looks down and sees the multitude of disagreements and all-out rows among His sons and daughters today. It was never meant to be this way! When he looks down on the splits and schisms, He must weep.

Many of us go to church with an awful attitude. Yet God wants our attitude to be just like our Elder Brother Jesus. (Philippians 2: 1-11) Jesus' command is 'Love one another' (John 13:34). And it is a command - not an optional extra. Love is the mark of the Christian, and this is how the world will know that we belong to God and follow Him- if we love one another.

We are to love and have 'koinonia' – deep fellowship with our brothers and sisters in Christ. Even those we don't like. Even those we clash with. Even those who make us feel inferior and awkward. Those we try to avoid. Those who make our blood boil. Those we annoy. Those who annoy us. Those who we find saying 'Hello' to more than enough!

Years ago, at a prayer meeting in Thailand, I heard a missionary, Nancy Hero say, "At the foot of the cross is level ground". It's such a true statement - we are all level and equal in God's eyes, in Christ. God has no favourites. He wants us to see others as He does - 'Discover beauty in everyone' (Romans 12:17-The Message) Love looks for the good in others and brings the best out in them!

Yet, often we treat others how they've treated us, rather than how we'd like to be treated - or more importantly how God wants us to treat them.

The New Testament is full of exhortations to guide us how to treat one another:

- 'Love one another deeply, from the heart'
(I Peter 1:22- NIV)
- 'Clothe yourselves with humility toward one another' (I Peter 5:5-NIV)
- 'Be completely humble and gentle, be patient, bearing with one another in love' (Ephesians 4:2 NIV) Or to put it another way: 'Be patient with each other, making allowance for each other's faults because of your love'
(Ephesians 4:2 – NLT)
- 'Be kind to each other, tenderhearted, forgiving one another, just as God through Christ has forgiven you' (Ephesians 4:32-NLT)
- 'Serve one another in love' (Galatians 5:13-NIV)
- 'Let us consider how we may spur one another on toward love and good deeds'
(Hebrews 10:24- NIV)
- 'So accept each other just as Christ has accepted you; then God will be glorified'
(Romans 15:7-NLT)
- 'Be devoted to one another in brotherly love. Honour one another above yourselves'
(Romans 12:10-NIV)
- 'Live in harmony with one another' (Romans 12:16-NIV) 'God's people should be big-hearted and courteous' (Titus 3:2- The Message)
- 'Each of you should look not only to your own interests, but also to the interests of others' (Philippians 2:4-NIV) 'Put yourself aside and help others get ahead' (Philippians 2: 3-The Message)

- 'Let the peace of Christ keep you in tune with each other, in step with each other'

  (Colossians 3:15-The Message)
- 'Do not judge, or you too will be judged' (Matthew 7:1-NIV) 'Never judge your neighbour until you've walked a mile in his moccasins!' (Old Indian proverb)
- 'Finally, all of you should be of one mind, full of sympathy toward each other, loving one another with tender hearts and humble minds.'

  (I Peter 3:8-NLT)

P.S. And for those of us who spend time deliberating what to wear to church, meditate on this verse: 'And the most important piece of clothing you must wear is love. Love is what binds us all together in perfect harmony' (Colossians 3:14-NLT) Indeed, no matter where we are, the most important piece of Designer clothing we can possess is love.

'Love from the centre of who you are, don't fake it' (Romans 12:9-The Message)

'Dear friends, since God loved us that much, we surely ought to love each other. No one has ever seen God. But if we love each other, God lives in us, and his love has been brought to full expression through us'

(I John 4:11&12-NLT)

'Let us stop just saying we love each other; let us really show it by our actions' (I John 3:18-NLT)

Love - the more we share it, the more it grows!

Loving others means encouraging them

Being a gift from God

Reading: Hebrews 10:19-25

> Encouragement means being a gift from God!
> Encouragement is like:
>
> - a ray of sunshine on a cold day
> - the warm glow of a fire
> - an oasis in the desert

There are 101 ways to encourage others- a cheerful greeting, a gentle hug, a quick text message, or e-mail, a little note, a hug, a loving touch, a sincere compliment, a surprise gift. A simple gesture can brighten our day!

I'll never forget one particular home visit I made in my last job in Mid-Ulster. After I'd finished, the lovely old lady led me through to the back of her terrace house to what I can only describe as an oasis- a garden teeming with roses. She carefully selected a few and sent me on my way with a bunch! I still smile when I think of her kindness- the feel-good effect has lasted years after the roses have withered and died.

When I was in hospital, people encouraged me in their own unique way- bringing flowers, bringing chocolates, bringing cranberry juice, bringing uplifting CDs, bringing a hug and just bringing themselves. Sending cards. Looking after the children. Looking after Rob. Taking me for out for coffee. Taking me for some retail therapy. Taking me to God, in prayer. Praying for me and mine when my head was too confused to pray for myself. God used those prayers more than we'll ever know.

Yet encouragement is even more than brightening someone's day - it is spurring them on. The Greek paraklesis literally means propelling someone in the right direction. Encouragement means to strengthen, uphold and comfort.

Never underestimate the power of words! One positive comment can keep us going with a spring in our step for days, while negative remarks can resound in our minds for years!

'Let us consider how we may spur one another on toward love and good deeds' (Hebrews 10:24 - NIV) 'Consider' means that we should actively look out for opportunities to encourage others. 'Think of ways to encourage one another to outbursts of love and good deeds'
(Hebrews 10:24-NLT)

'Gently encourage the stragglers, and reach out for the exhausted, pulling them to their feet. Be patient with each person, attentive to their individual needs'
(I Thessalonians 5:13-The Message)

'Look for the best in each other, and always do your best to bring it out'   (I Thessalonians 5:15-The Message)

'Cheerfully share your home with those who need a meal or place to stay' (I Peter 4:9-NLT)

'Therefore encourage one another and build each other up, just as in fact you are doing.'
(I Thessalonians 5:11-NIV)

'Your love has given me great joy and encouragement, because you have refreshed the hearts of the saints'
(Philemon 1:7 - NIV)

May my heart be full of the sunshine of God's love- whatever the weather!

Loving others means seeing the world through God's eyes

Being a world-wide Christian!

Reading: Matthew 25: 31-46

'For God so loved the world', the famous verse John 3:16 begins. God loves the world, the whole world. Yet so often we can't see beyond ourselves, our family, our church, our neighbourhood.

I don't think I really grasped how much our God loves the whole world until summer of '95. I went on an OM Love Europe Mission with my friend Beth. In Budapest, George Verwer, founder of OM, urged us to pray for the world and to go into the world, as he held a giant inflatable globe in his hands. The next week, while on an international OM team in the Czech Republic, we gathered round a world map to pray. Members of the team were from far-flung places like Ecuador, USA, Finland, Czech Republic and of course the UK. As I looked at the map, I noticed that Northern Ireland was little more than a crease on the world map - so tiny compared to other countries, just one little part of our planet, God's planet. Yet how often we act like the whole world revolves round us and ours!

At that same OM conference in 1995, a speaker said "Ask God what is breaking His heart and ask Him to break yours in the same place." The next year, when I went to Thailand on my elective, God showed me what was breaking His heart there, and I was heartbroken too. People bowing prostrate before man-made idols, instead of our God, the one true God broke His heart. Babies in a Bangkok orphanage, orphaned because of AIDS (and now suffering more as they were HIV positive too) surely must break the Father-heart of God.

What is breaking God's heart in our world today?

We must see His world through His eyes- as we look across the street and across the globe. 'When Jesus saw the crowds, he had compassion on them, because they were harassed and helpless, like sheep without a shepherd.' (Matthew 9:36 NIV) The original word, translated as compassion is splanchnomazia – literally feeling another's hurt in our heart. Our attitude should be the same as Jesus'. We must ask W.W.J.D? -what would Jesus do? For, we are His hands, feet and voice today, and as today's reading reminds us "Whatever you did for the least of these, you did it for me" (Matthew 25:40 - NIV) 'Never walk away from someone who deserves help; your hand is *God's* hand for that person'

(Proverbs 3:27-The Message)

Often we think the only missionaries are those who leave for far-off lands. And I'm sure many of us have spent prolonged periods of time believing that God wanted us to go overseas. We've had many somewhat romantic ideas of what life would be like, and we've been disappointed when God has guided us to stay at home. Yet home is sometimes more difficult - in different ways. I know I truly believed that I'd be back in Thailand as a medical missionary by the time I was 30. Yet here, at home, people who speak my language and share my culture, surround me yet I find it so difficult to share my faith.

A few years ago, at the Worldwide Missionary Convention in Bangor, Stuart Briscoe gave a very refreshing talk about being Home **and** Away Christians. We shouldn't feel disappointed because we're not 'Away', but ask God to open the eyes of our heart to every God given opportunity. In Acts 1:8, Luke wrote how Jesus said that the disciples would be His witnesses in Jerusalem, and in all Judea and Samaria, and to the ends of the earth. Starting at home, in our local area and extending in ever-increasing circles, as wide as the world itself, far away, we can serve God. We get hung up on geography-but God wants us to serve Him wherever we are, with whatever we've got.

'Start where you are, use what you've got, and do the best you can for Jesus!' (Mike Mullins OM- speaking at Worldwide 2005)

Not long after I became a Christian, when I was almost 14, I read this quote (I can't remember where!) and wrote it into my Bible: 'Every heart with Christ, a missionary, every heart without Christ a mission-field' Wow-that gets things into perspective!

And the need is so great. 'In a world pushing towards 6 billion people, we must face the reality that many have still not heard the Gospel, much less have a church or witness in their midst' (George Verwer)[7]

We can pray, give and go as the need and opportunity arises. We can change the world 'one life at a time' by sponsoring a child with an organisation like Compassion. We can make a difference to the world's poor by supporting Tearcraft. We can fill shoeboxes with gifts for those who won't get anything else at Christmas. We can pray for missionaries and support them. And we can ask God what is breaking His heart and ask Him to break ours in the same place.

'True spirituality has one eye on the scriptures and one eye on the newspaper, one ear open to God's voice and one alert to the cries of His world, one hand raised in prayer and intercession, the other reaching out to care and serve in the strength God supplies.' (Author unknown)

'Whoever is kind to the needy honours God'
(Proverbs 14:31- NIV)

'She opens her arms to the poor and extends her hands to the needy' (Proverbs 31:20 -NIV)

'Real religion, the kind that passes muster before God the Father is this: Reach out to the homeless and loveless in their plight.' (James 1:27-The Message)

'Anyone, then, who knows the good he ought to do, and doesn't do it, sins' (James 4:17-NIV) *'Doing nothing is as bad as doing wrong'*
'When God's children are in need, be the one to help them out' (Romans 12:13-NLT)

'The only thing that counts is faith expressing itself through love' (Galatians 5:6-NIV)

'Love is an active verb!'

God,

Help me to do what you've planned for me to do, to become all that you want me to be, to grow deeper and deeper into you, and to fall more and more in love with you.

I want to know your heartbeat and to serve your purpose in my generation.

Help me to respond to your inner promptings and make the most of every opportunity.

I want to make a difference and to have eternal impact on those I meet along life's path. May I make everlasting impressions on those you bring into my life.

May I encourage Your church and add to it.

May Your love flow through me to others, that they may see You in me, that Your Name would be lifted high and Your family extended.

May I live a life of love.

Amen!

'May the peoples praise you, O God; may all the peoples praise you.'   (Psalm 67:3-NIV)

Conclusion

It's all about love! For, God first loved us and poured His amazing, unending, extravagant love into our lives.

It's all about love!

- Loving God with all that we've got.
- Loving and helping our husbands.
- Loving our children and nurturing them in a loving home.
- Loving and serving God's people
- Loving and reaching out into God's world - with a love like His!

We are to be imitators of God. The Greek word for imitate literally means mimic- i.e. copy His actions, echo His speech and follow His example.

'Be imitators of God, therefore, as dearly loved children and live a life of love, just as Christ loved us and gave Himself up for us as a fragrant offering and sacrifice to God'   (Ephesians 5:1&2 - NIV)

God bless- and He will!

An Irish Blessing

May the road rise to meet you
May the wind be always at your back
May the sun shine always
Upon your face
The rains fall soft upon your fields
And until we meet again
May God hold you
In the hollow of His hand

(Traditional)

'May the Lord smile on you
and be gracious to you.
May the Lord show you his favour
and give you his peace' (Numbers 6:25&26-NLT)

'May you be blessed by the Lord,
the Maker of heaven and earth' (Psalm 115:15- NIV)

How to become a Christian

I'm assuming that most people reading this book would already consider themselves to be Christians. But maybe you have read this book and you are not a Christian, and you are wondering how to become a Christian-how to have the personal relationship with God that's been described in this book.

Many leaflets and books have been written about this subject. While becoming a Christian is a life- changing event, sometimes I think we make it sound more complicated than God ever intended it to be! Indeed, God wants us to have child-like faith. And becoming a Christian comes down to praying and telling God those little words that we try to teach our children to say – sorry, thank you and please.

We need to say **sorry** (and really mean it) for all the wrong things we've done, realising that these things hurt God.

We need to say **thank you** to God for loving us so much that he sent Jesus to die on the cross, to take the punishment for the wrong things we've done.

We need to say **please** and ask God to forgive us, and help us to live our lives for Him.

"Now its time to change your ways! Turn to face God so he can wipe away your sins, pour out showers of blessing to refresh yo, and send you the Messiah he prepared for you, namely, Jesus."

(Acts 3:17 The Message)

'May you hear His voice and return His love with your life' (Angela Thomas)[1]

Love's Response- Studies for personal reflection and group discussion

1-The love of God

Reading- Ephesians 3:14-21

- What is the most amazing aspect of God's love for us?
- In the book I wrote that it wasn't the nails that kept Jesus on the cross, but His love for you and me. Do you agree?
- Do you find it easy to go into 'God's laundry room' for cleansing and forgiveness?
- How can we celebrate the gift of today?
- How can we stop worrying and just trust God for the future?
- The love of God means that we are daughters of the King. How does that make you feel?

Pray- Thank God for His amazing love

Reflect- How can you say thank you to God this week with your life?

2-Loving God

Readings- Matthew 6:33&34, Romans 5:1-5

- How many Names of God can you think of? What aspect of His character is revealed in each Name?
- Jesus said I AM 'the bread of life' (John 6:35), 'the light of the world' (8:12), 'the gate' (10:9), 'the good shepherd' (10:11), 'the resurrection and the life' (11:25), 'the way, the truth and the life' (14:6) and 'the true vine' (15:5) How do you find comfort in all that Jesus says He is?
- What practical steps can we take to slow down and draw near to God? How can we choose what is best and keep our love for Him alive?
- If the Bible is food to nourish our souls why do we starve ourselves?
- 'Loving God means learning to love ourselves' Why do we find this difficult despite being truly blessed by God?
- If God's mighty power is at work in us (Ephesians 1:19), why do we so often choose to do things on our own?
- Have there been times when life hurt? Share how you felt and how God helped you through. Was it difficult to wait for God's timing-for winter to be over and for spring to begin?

Pray- Thank God for His help in the tough times

Reflect- 'He who is richest is rich in God's love'

3-Love in the home

Readings – Titus 2:4&5, Ephesians 5

- In what practical ways can we show our husbands that we understand and support them?
- Stormie Omartian wrote 'Part of making a house a home is allowing your husband to be the head, so that you can be the heart' do you agree?
- Do you think that loving your children does mean asking God for help?
- Share any 'teachable moments' that you've shared with your children recently.
- What measures can we take to make our house a true home?

Pray- Spend time thanking God for the family God has given you. Pray for their needs.

Reflect- 'A mother's love is the heart of a home'

4-Loving others

Reading- John 13

- Are you a vase or a bucket? How can we refresh others?
- Prayer is a direct line to our Father in Heaven. Why do we use prayer much less than we use our mobile phones?
- Share ways that others have encouraged you. How can we encourage others?
- How can we treat one another the way God would want us to?
- How can we see the world through God's eyes?
- How can we show His love across the globe without leaving home?

Pray - Take time to pray for one another. Ask God to show you how you can show His love- across the street and across the world!

Reflect- We are blessed to be a blessing!

A goody bag!

My kids love parties! But for Ethan, the **very** best part of the party is the goody bag given out at the end!

If I was giving you a goody bag, at the end of this book, what would be in it?

A little cross - a reminder that God is love. At the beginning of all, is His love. He loved so much that He gave. He gave His Son, and He gives us all that we need. He gives and He keeps on giving.

A washing powder tablet - to remind us that God has cleansed our past, our failings and that each time we mess up we need another visit to his laundry room!

A dressing up tiara- to remind us, that we ARE princesses- because we're daughters of the King of kings.

A scented candle - to remind us that we are to leave the aroma of Jesus and shine His light -just where we are.

A packet of love heart sweets- because it's all about love!

Notes

Part 1- The love of God

1. Copyright InTouch Ministries. Stoneman, Tonya, *Eternity in Every Moment*, In Touch Magazine, March 2001. www.intouch.org
2. Reprinted by permission. A Beautiful Offering, Angela Thomas, 2004, Thomas Nelson Inc. Nashville, Tennessee. All rights reserved.
3. WE HAVE THIS MOMENT, TODAY – Words by Gloria Gaither. Music by William J. Gaither. Copyright © 1975 William J. Gaither, Inc. All rights controlled by Gaither Copyright Management. Used by permission.
4. Excerpt taken from: Just Enough Light for the Step I'm on
   Copyright © 1999 by Stormie Omartian
   Published by Harvest House Publishers, Eugene, OR
   Used by Permission
5. © 2002 Day Spring Cards, Inc
6. Excerpt taken from: Sermons of Robert Murray M'Cheyne
   Published by The Banner of Truth Trust, 3 Murrayfield Road, Edinburgh, EH12 6EL
   www.banneroftruth.org

Part 2- Loving God

1. Taken from The Purpose-Driven Life by Rick Warren
   Copyright © 2002 by Rick Warren
   Used by permission of Zondervan
2. Reprinted by permission. A Gentle Thunder, Max Lucado, 2001,Thomas Nelson Inc, Nashville, Tennessee. All rights reserved
3. From The Word For Today, United Christian Broadcasters, PO Box 255, Stoke-on-Trent, ST4 8YY, England. www.ucb.co.uk
   Free issues of this daily devotional are available for the UK and Republic of Ireland
4. Reprinted by permission. A Beautiful Offering, Angela Thomas, 2004, Thomas Nelson Inc. Nashville, Tennesee. All rights reserved.

Part 3- Loving others

1. Excerpt taken from: The Power of a Praying Wife
   Copyright © 1997 by Stormie Omartian
   Published by Harvest House Publishers, Eugene, OR
   Used by Permission
2. From: The Five Love Languages of Children
   Published by Moody Publishers, Chicago, 1997
   Dr. Gary Chapman and Ross Campbell, MD are co-authors of this book.
3. The twenty-first century supermum © Christine Orme, from Just a Minute published by Scripture Union, Bletchley, bucks, MK2 2EB
4. Taken from Fresh Elastic for Stretched out Moms
   Copyright © 1986 by Barbara Johnson, published by Fleming H Revell. A division of Baker Book House Company

P.O. Box 6287, Grand Rapids, Michigan 49516-6287
5. Taken from Every Child needs a Praying Mom by Fern Nichols
   Copyright © 2003 by Fern Nichols
   Used by permission of Zondervan
6. East Asia's Billions (July-Sept 2004)- the quarterly magazine of Overseas Missionary Fellowship (OMF International) E-mail omf@omf.org.uk www.omf.org.uk
7. George Verwer, founder of Operation Mobilisation- quoted with permission

How to become a Christian

1. Reprinted by permission. A Beautiful Offering, Angela Thomas, 2004, Thomas Nelson Inc. Nashville, Tennesee. All rights reserved.

Recommended reading

Loving God

The purpose driven life, Rick Warren, Zondervan, 2002
   If you haven't read this book, why not? Grab a copy today, and rediscover what on earth you're here for!

I wanna be a woman of God! Beth Redman, Hodder & Stoughton 2005
   An up to date look at how to live for God in the noughties!

A beautiful offering, Angela Thomas, Nelson Books 2004
   A refreshing view of the Sermon on the Mount, and how our aim should be to return God's love with our lives.

A woman after God's own heart, Elizabeth George, Harvest House Publishers, 2007 (updated and expanded edition)
   'Become the woman of excellence God designed you to be'

Loving yourself

Captivating, John & Stasi Eldredge, Nelson Books 2005
   A unique book that seeks to unveil the mystery of a

women's soul. It reminds us that God wants to release us to live as fully alive, feminine women.

Life management for busy women, Elizabeth George, Harvest House Publishers 2002
'Living out God's plan with passion and purpose'

The power of a praying woman, Stormie Omartian, Harvest House Publishers 2007
Praying to God about yourself- so that you become more like the women He created you to be.

Loving your husband

The Marriage Book, Nicky & Sila Lee, Alpha International 2000
How to build a healthy marriage that lasts a lifetime

Becoming the woman of his dreams, Sharon Jaynes, Harvest House Publishers 2005
A look at the unique, God-ordained role you have in your husband's life, and the qualities he longs for you to possess.

The power of a praying wife, Stormie Omartian, Harvest House Publishers 2007
Develop a deeper relationship with your husband by praying for him.

The five love languages, Gary Chapman, Northfield Publishing 1992
How to express your love in a 'language' that your husband will understand and appreciate.

Loving your children - for mums and moms!

Every Child needs a Praying Mom, Fern Nichols, Zondervan 2005
A book about the power of prayer and the everlasting impact it can have on the lives of our children.

Just a minute, Christine Orme, Scripture Union 2001
Biblical reflections for busy mums

Tender Mercies for a mother's soul, Angela Thomas, Tyndale House 2006
Take time out to nurture you relationship with god as you care for your family.

When times are tough

Blessed be your name, Matt & Beth Redman, Hodder & Stoughton 2005
This is the story behind the song that became an anthem for me when life hurt and things were difficult. It focuses on worshipping God on the road marked with suffering.

Life is tough but God is faithful, Sheila Walsh, Thomas Nelson 1999
I read this book during my second hospital stay. It goes through Job's trials, and deals with how to see God's love in difficult times. The valuable conclusion is that knowing God is better than knowing answers.

Fiction

Even now, Karen Kingsbury, Zondervan 2005 'a soul-stirring tale of lost love and forgiveness..' and the sequel:

Ever After, Karen Kingsbury, Zondervan 2006

'A powerful tale of patriotism, undying love, and the true power of sacrifice.'

These are no ordinary stories- they are Life Changing Fiction TM. And make sure you have some tissues handy!

Useful websites

www.careforthefamily.org.uk
Care for the family- strengthening family life and helping those who are hurting due to family breakdown.

www.compassion.org
Compassion-by sponsoring a child, you can change the world one life at a time!

www.coolrunning.com
The star spot on this site has to be the 'couch-to-5K' running plan! For couch potatoes that want to get running again!

www.messiesanonymous.com
Helpful hints for an organised house!
But those of us who are Messy with a capital M, only need to go to this site when-

(1) Your own bedroom is messier than your kids' rooms!
(2) You can't find a matching pair of **your own** shoes in the morning!
(3) Your ironing pile is taller than your youngest child!

www.momsense.com
Mom sense- Christianity Today's parenting website-
'because mothering matters!' You can subscribe to a
weekly e-zine with many thought-provoking articles!

www.omf.org.uk
Overseas Missionary Fellowship -bringing hope in hard
places- serving the church and bringing the Gospel to 12
countries in South Asia.

www.om.org.uk
Operation Mobilisation- Bringing hope to the peoples
of the world. This missionary organisation works in
over 100 countries. (The UK homepage can be found at
www.uk.om.org)

www.tearfund.org
Tearfund - be part of a miracle! Their 10yr vision is to
see 50 million people released from material and spiritual poverty through a worldwide network of 100,000
local churches!

www.ucb.co.uk
United Christian Broadcasters- changing lives for good
via evangelism, discipleship and mission. Free copies of
the daily devotional Word for Today are available,
along with other resources

God's love in action
at House of Grace

I want to use the last page of the book to share about a project that is close to my heart- the House of Grace Child Foundation, Chantaburi, 150 miles south-east of Bangkok, Thailand.

In 1998, House of Grace began when Pastor Kitisak and his wife Jariya, with their 2 daughters, opened their home to two orphans who had no-one to care for them. By 2001 Kitisak and his growing family moved to live in an abandoned school building.

In April 2003,Kitisak became guardian to the children at the House of Grace and in December 2005, the House of Grace Child Foundation (HGCF) was legally registered.

There are now 50 children living at House of Grace (some are HIV +) In Autumn 2007 they hope to move to new purpose built premises!

The goals of House of Grace are:

- To provide a loving home environment for orphans affected by AIDS where each child can continue their education, receive care, a Christian upbringing and be guided into membership of the local church.

- To provide a temporary safe refuge to mothers with AIDS where they are accepted, receive support, encouragement and help in caring for themselves.
- To assist other children affected by HIV/AIDS to remain living with their family at home and continue their education as long as possible.
- To provide young people in the community with knowledge and life skills in order to prevent them from becoming infected with HIV.

To support this project and/or to find out more-

Email: *ACET.houseofgrace@gmail.com*

Website: www.houseofgracethailand.com

Printed in the United Kingdom
by Lightning Source UK Ltd.
125423UK00001B/7-78/A